GCSE OCR B Religious Studies

Philosophy 1 & 2

The Revision Guide

Want to hear the **bad news**? There's an awful lot of heavy-going stuff they expect you to learn for GCSE Religious Studies.

Want to hear the **good news**? Good old CGP have got it all covered! We've produced this brilliant book, with all the key concepts explained in clear, simple English so you can understand it — and remember it.

And then, in the spirit of going the extra mile, we've put in a smattering of not-so-serious bits to try and make the whole experience at least partly entertaining for you.

We've done all we can — the rest is up to you.

What CGP is all about

Our sole aim here at CGP is to produce the highest quality books — carefully written, immaculately presented and dangerously close to being funny.

Then we work our socks off to get them out to you — at the cheapest possible prices.

Contents

Guide to Symbols

This book covers both Philosophy Units in the context of **Christianity**, **Islam** and **Judaism**.
The clouds in the corners of the pages tell you whether the page covers:

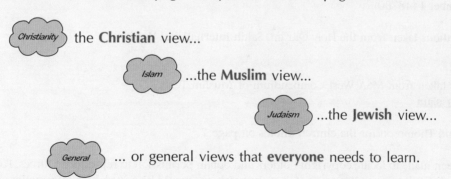

Christianity the **Christian** view...

Islam ...the **Muslim** view...

Judaism ...the **Jewish** view...

General ... or general views that **everyone** needs to learn.

Bible / Qur'an References

References from the Bible always go in the order: **Book Chapter:Verse(s)**.
So whenever you see something like: **Mark 3:5-6**, it means it's from the
book of Mark, Chapter 3, Verses 5-6.

Similarly, references from the Qur'an are shown with the **Surah (Chapter)**
followed by the **Ayat (Verse)**.

Published by Coordination Group Publications Ltd

Editors:
Luke von Kotze, Andy Park, Julie Wakeling

Contributors:
Stewart Bates, Jill Hudson, Duncan Raynor, Paul D. Smith, Nigel Thomas

ISBN: 978 1 84762 348 5

With thanks to Mary Falkner and Karen Gascoigne for the proofreading.
With thanks to Laura Phillips for the copyright research.

Biblical quotations taken from the HOLY BIBLE, NEW INTERNATIONAL VERSION
Copyright © 1973, 1978, 1984 by International Bible Society
All rights reserved.
"NIV" is a registered trademark of the International Bible Society.
UK trademark number 1448790

Holy Qur'an quotations taken from the Holy Qur'an, Sahih International Version
www.quran.com

Hadith quotations taken from MSA West Compendium of Muslim Texts
www.msawest.net/islam

With thanks to Enid Thompson for the church photos on page 7.

Groovy website: www.cgpbooks.co.uk

Jolly bits of clipart from CorelDRAW®
Printed by Elanders Ltd, Newcastle upon Tyne

Based on the classic CGP style created by Richard Parsons.

Photocopying – it's dull, grey and sometimes a bit naughty. Luckily, it's dead cheap, easy and quick to order more copies of this book from CGP – just call us on 0870 750 1242. Phew!

The Nature of God

Welcome to GCSE Religious Studies — I guess the best place to start is with God.
Who is that, I hear you wonder. Well, that's a tricky one...

What's God Like? — The Debate Continues...

The question of <u>what God is like</u> has occupied religious thinkers for <u>hundreds of years</u>.
There are three main issues:

> 1) Is God a kind of '<u>person</u>' or a kind of '<u>force</u>'?
> 2) Is God <u>within or outside</u> the Universe?
> 3) Is there just <u>one god</u> or are there <u>many gods</u>?

None of these ideas are without problems, however, and many
people would argue that God is actually a combination of them all.

Is God a 'Person'?

1) The term '<u>personal god</u>' refers to God as a '<u>person</u>' — albeit an almighty and <u>divine person</u>.
   God would be someone that <u>supports and cares</u> for us <u>as a friend</u> would, with <u>human emotions</u> like us.
   If this were the case, <u>prayer</u> would become part of our individual relationship — a '<u>conversation</u>' with God.

2) The problem with this is that God is meant to be <u>omnipresent</u> (everywhere at once) —
   which poses the question of <u>how</u> a <u>personal god</u> can be <u>everywhere at once</u>.

3) The term '<u>impersonal god</u>' refers to God as a <u>concept</u>, a <u>force</u> or an <u>idea</u>
   of <u>goodness and light</u>. The '<u>prime number</u>' theory is often used to
   represent this idea of God — something that <u>can't be divided</u> or reduced.

4) The <u>obvious problem</u> here is how you can have a <u>relationship</u> with a <u>force</u> or an <u>idea</u>.

Where is God?

1) An '<u>immanent</u>' God is a God who is <u>in the world</u> with us — a God who has taken an <u>active role</u> in the
   progress of <u>human history</u> and <u>continues</u> to do so.

2) The <u>problem</u> here is that an immanent God may appear <u>small</u> and <u>fallible</u>.

3) On the other hand, a '<u>transcendent</u>' God is <u>outside the world</u> and <u>doesn't directly act</u> in human
   history.

4) This view of God makes him <u>remote</u> and <u>separate</u> from our experience on Earth. However, <u>Christians</u>
   who see God as transcendent might argue that it is <u>they</u> who <u>do the work</u> of God and that he is
   working <u>through them</u>.

5) Unfortunately, this definition is a bit <u>too abstract</u> for a lot of people to understand.

6) Religious believers (and Christians in particular) often try <u>not</u> to deal with <u>extremes</u> of any of these
   ideas, preferring instead to draw on <u>different aspects</u> for different occasions. Many would argue that
   God needs to be a <u>blend</u> of all of the above.

How Many Gods are There?

1) <u>Monotheism</u> is the idea of <u>one God</u>.
   This exists in <u>Christianity</u>, <u>Judaism</u> and <u>Islam</u>.

2) <u>Polytheism</u> is the belief in <u>more than one</u> god,
   e.g. in Classical Greek and Roman civilisations,
   and some forms of Hinduism.

> *Although Christianity is monotheistic, there is a belief
> that God is actually <u>three in one</u> (the <u>Trinity</u> — see p.2)
> — the <u>Father</u>, the <u>Son</u> (Jesus) and the <u>Holy Spirit</u>.*

One for sorrow, two for joy... three for a girl... four for a boy...

This is seriously <u>tricky</u> stuff — and not just for Religious Studies. These questions have been worrying <u>loads</u>
of people for <u>ages</u>. But, tricky or not, you have to understand all these arguments to do well in that GCSE.

Christianity & Judaism

Beliefs About God

There are many <u>different ideas</u> about what a god is. But Christian, Jewish and Muslim beliefs are quite <u>similar</u>.

Judaism and Christianity say Similar Things about God...

1) As <u>Christianity</u> grew <u>directly from Judaism</u>, the <u>basic concept</u> of God is something the <u>two faiths share</u>.

2) The Judeo-Christian God is <u>usually seen as male</u> (referred to as He or Father) although nowadays many religious believers would argue that this is simply because when these religions were founded society was male-dominated, and that God is actually neither male nor female.

3) <u>Both faiths</u> share the ideas that God is omnipotent (<u>all-powerful</u>), omnipresent (<u>everywhere</u>) and omniscient (<u>all-knowing</u>), that God is <u>divine</u>, <u>supreme</u>, <u>totally good</u> and <u>totally perfect</u>, and that God has given us <u>free will</u>.

However, many Jews and Christians believe that our lives are <u>predestined</u> — we control <u>individual actions</u>, but not the <u>ultimate outcome</u> of our lives.

...but There are Some Big Differences

4) The <u>biggest difference</u> is the <u>Christian belief</u> in the <u>Trinity</u>. Jews <u>never believed Christ</u> was the <u>Son of God</u>.

5) Another key difference between Jewish and Christian teaching is that <u>Jews</u> are <u>forbidden</u> to draw or <u>make images</u> of <u>God</u>.

"Hear O Israel: the Lord our God, the Lord is One"

Jews don't <u>all</u> believe exactly the same things. They have many different opinions on many important issues. Most believe these 11 things about God. They believe <u>God is</u>...

...ONE   Jews believe there's only one God. The heading above comes from <u>Deuteronomy 6:4</u> — it's the opening of a very important Jewish prayer called the <u>Shema</u>.

...A PERSON   i.e. he's not just a 'force', but neither is he an old man with a beard. Human beings were made '<u>in his image</u>' (but this needn't mean he looks like us).

...THE CREATOR   i.e. he made the Universe and everything in it. Jews don't invent clever arguments for God's existence — they say that creation makes it <u>obvious</u> that he's there.

...THE SUSTAINER   i.e. he didn't just create the Universe and then sit back — his <u>energy</u> keeps it going.

...HOLY   'Holy' means '<u>set apart</u>' or '<u>completely pure</u>'. God (or <u>YHWH</u> in Hebrew) is so holy that some Jews won't even write or say the word 'God' — they write <u>G-d</u> and say <u>Hashem</u> ('the Name') or <u>Adonai</u> ('the Lord', or 'the Master').

...OMNIPOTENT   i.e. <u>all-powerful</u> — although he still allows each person <u>free will</u>.

...OMNISCIENT   i.e. he <u>knows everything</u>, even your darkest secrets and your wildest dreams.

...OMNIPRESENT   i.e. present throughout the <u>whole Universe</u>.

...THE LAWGIVER   Jewish tradition says '<u>God wrote himself into the Torah</u>'.

...THE TRUE JUDGE   Jews believe they shall all face him one day, for death is <u>not</u> 'the end'.

...THE REDEEMER   Jews believe God is <u>merciful</u>. He will <u>save</u> his people from sin and suffering.

The Trinity is Explained Nicely in the Nicene Creed

1) The <u>Christian</u> idea of the <u>Trinity</u> is perhaps best expressed in the <u>Nicene Creed</u>:

> *"We believe in one God, the Father, the almighty, maker of heaven and earth... We believe in one Lord, Jesus Christ, the only son of God... Of one being with the Father... We believe in the Holy Spirit... The giver of life... Who proceeds from the Father and the Son..."*

2) <u>God the Father</u> might be described as the <u>transcendent part</u> of God, the <u>Son</u> as the <u>immanent</u> and <u>personal</u> part, and the <u>Holy Spirit</u> the <u>immanent yet impersonal</u> (see page 1).

3) Similarly, Christians might describe the <u>Father</u> as the <u>creator</u> and <u>judge</u>, the <u>Son</u> (Jesus) as the <u>human incarnation</u> of God (and the <u>Messiah</u>, or saviour), and the <u>Holy Spirit</u> as the <u>force of God</u> — inspiring, guiding and comforting them.

Beliefs About Allah

Islam <u>shares</u> a lot of history and beliefs with Judaism and Christianity.
But Muslims believe Islam is the "<u>final word of god</u>".

The Muslim name for God is Allah

1) For Muslims, God is called <u>Allah</u> — and the word '<u>Islam</u>' can
be translated as meaning '<u>submission</u>' or '<u>surrender</u>' to Allah.

2) According to Islamic teaching, <u>Allah</u> is the <u>creator</u> of everything.

3) He is referred to by <u>ninety-nine names</u> in the Qur'an — these names
tell you what <u>Muslims believe</u> about Allah and his power. They include:
<u>Ar-Khaliq</u> — The <u>Creator</u>, <u>Ar-Rahman</u> — The <u>Merciful</u>, <u>Ar-Aziz</u> — The <u>Almighty</u>.
He is also called The <u>Provider</u>, The <u>Just</u>, The <u>Maintainer</u>, The <u>Hearer</u> and The <u>Real Truth</u>.

"He is Allah, the One, Allah is Eternal and Absolute"

1) This passage is taken from Surah 112 and describes the <u>basic principle</u> that <u>Allah is one</u>.
Islam is a <u>monotheistic</u> religion (see page 1) and this belief in the oneness
or the <u>unity of Allah</u> (called <u>Tawhid</u>) is a <u>fundamental</u> principle of Islam.

2) The ninety-nine names sum up much of the nature of Allah. He is <u>loving</u> and <u>compassionate</u>,
he is the <u>creator</u> and <u>judge</u> of all humans, and knows <u>everything</u> they do.

3) Muslims believe Allah <u>cannot</u> be thought of in human terms — he is the <u>Supreme Being</u> and has <u>no equal</u>.

4) To Muslims, Allah is <u>both immanent</u> and <u>transcendent</u> (see page 1).
He is <u>transcendent</u> in that he is the <u>power behind the Universe</u> and is <u>outside</u>, above or beyond
both <u>his creation</u> and <u>time</u> itself. His <u>immanence</u> is demonstrated in this passage:
*"And We have already created man and <u>know</u> what his soul whispers to him,
and We are closer to him than [his] <u>jugular vein</u>."* Qur'an 50:16
(In this passage 'We' refers to Allah and 'him' or 'his' refers to humankind.)

5) Human lives are <u>predestined</u> by Allah — but humans do have <u>free will</u> (see page 19).

There are Five Main Ways to Know Allah

1) Muslims believe that Allah has <u>intervened</u> in <u>human history</u> and that this is one way of
<u>knowing</u> him and <u>his power</u>. His message was delivered by the <u>prophets</u>, of whom
twenty-five are mentioned in the Qur'an. These include <u>Musa</u> (<u>Moses</u>) and '<u>Isa</u> (<u>Jesus</u>).
The last was the Prophet <u>Muhammad</u>, who <u>brought Allah's message</u> to the people.

2) Allah has also performed <u>miracles</u> (see p.5).

3) The <u>Five Pillars of Islam</u> also provide opportunities to know and be close to Allah.
These are: <u>Shahadah</u> (a statement of <u>belief</u>),
<u>Salah</u> (<u>prayer</u>) — see p.13.
<u>Zakah</u> (<u>charitable</u> duty),
<u>Sawm</u> (<u>fasting</u>),
<u>Hajj</u> (<u>pilgrimage</u>).

Muslim prayer ritual
— see page 13.

4) Muslims believe that the <u>Qur'an</u> is the <u>word of Allah</u> and allows humans to know him.
Many Muslims learn it off by heart, and all try to live according to the guidelines found within it.

5) Muslims believe Allah is good and kind. However, there is a belief in a <u>devil</u> (called <u>Iblis</u> or <u>Shaytan</u>)
who was <u>cast out by Allah</u> and tries to <u>lead people away</u> from him. <u>Some</u> Muslims would argue that
Allah <u>allows Shaytan</u> to use this power to <u>test and tempt</u> us — we have the <u>free will to resist</u>.

Immanent AND transcendent? — I Qur'an't get my head round it...

There's some <u>mind-boggling stuff</u> in these last few pages about what (one or more) god(s) is/are. But at the
end of the day, it seems Christians, Jews and Muslims <u>all agree</u> on the <u>fundamentals</u> — that God/Allah is <u>divine</u>,
<u>supreme</u>, <u>all-powerful</u> and <u>all-knowing</u>, that our <u>lives are predestined</u> by him/her/it and that we have <u>free will</u>.

Reasons For Belief

Millions of people across the world believe in some kind of <u>divine being</u> or '<u>god</u>'. They believe for various reasons — for some people, it's based on <u>personal religious experience</u>, but for others it's more <u>indirect</u>. For many people, the fact that they're <u>brought up</u> in a religious environment leads to or supports belief in a god.

It Can Start with Your Upbringing or a Search for Meaning

1) People brought up by <u>religious parents</u> and given <u>religious teaching</u> are <u>more likely</u> to <u>believe</u> in a god. The same is true for those brought up in a <u>religious community</u> where life's based on faith in one particular religion.

2) The presence of <u>religion in the world</u> gives some people faith, based on the <u>good work</u> that religion does — whether it be for <u>individuals</u>, <u>communities</u> or those who are experiencing <u>suffering</u>.

3) Some people are drawn to the <u>purpose</u> and <u>structure</u> it provides — or simply to the desire to have <u>something to believe in</u>.

4) Some people's faith is strengthened by the <u>feelings</u> they experience during <u>worship</u>. For some it's an <u>awareness</u> of the <u>presence</u> of god. Others, such as those involved in 'charismatic' worship, have more extreme experiences such as dancing, <u>speaking in tongues</u> (unknown languages) or uncontrollable shaking and crying.

5) The <u>search for meaning</u> is a major reason for people becoming interested in a particular religion. People want to find <u>answers</u> or find out why life is as it is, and they might believe religion can help. Becoming a follower of a religion in this way is called <u>conversion</u>.

6) This desire to find out <u>why we are here</u> or <u>why bad things happen</u> in the world might also <u>explain</u> why some people <u>move from one religion</u> to another.

Someone Must Have Designed the Planet

1) Many people are convinced by what are known as '<u>design' arguments</u> — the idea that the <u>intricate workings</u> of the <u>Universe</u> (or of <u>life</u>) <u>can't</u> have come about by <u>random chance</u>. There must have been some kind of <u>designer</u> and this designer was <u>God</u>.

2) Isaac Newton's <u>thumb theory</u> (*because every <u>thumbprint</u> is intricate and <u>unique</u>, there must be a God*) and William Paley's <u>watchmaker theory</u> (*you <u>wouldn't think</u> an <u>intricate watch</u> you found was made <u>by chance</u> — so why believe the <u>world was</u>*) are both design arguments.

3) Even Albert Einstein, one of the most prominent scientists of the twentieth century, said: *"When I see all the glories of the cosmos, I can't help but believe that there is a <u>divine hand</u> behind it all."*

4) Einstein might have been talking about design, but this might also be interpreted as a reference to a '<u>numinous</u>' experience — something which <u>inspires awe and wonder</u> at God's creation.

5) Other people are convinced by '<u>causation' arguments</u>. Our Universe works on the principle of 'cause and effect' — i.e. everything that happens is caused by something else. Some people argue that this chain must have started with an uncaused cause, or a '<u>First Cause</u>', and that this First Cause was <u>God</u>.

6) <u>Miracles</u> (see p.5) and the <u>power of prayer</u> (p.12-13) might also lead someone to believe in God, but these are <u>directly religious</u> reasons which we'll look at later.

7) However, some of the <u>non-religious ideas</u> about the origin of the world might lead someone to become an <u>agnostic</u> (someone who believes it's <u>impossible to know</u> whether there's a god or not) or an <u>atheist</u> (someone who <u>rejects completely</u> the idea of a divine being).

8) There's more about the relationship between <u>religion and science</u> in Philosophy 2 (see page 36).

A lot to learn here? You'd better believe it...

Basically, <u>religion</u>'s a <u>personal</u> thing — Bob believes cos <u>his mum</u> does, Sam <u>gazes at the stars</u> at night and reckons there <u>must be a god</u>, and Al <u>doesn't</u> believe <u>at all</u>. <u>Learn all these reasons</u> for believing — you <u>get marks</u> for <u>including them</u> in your answers. Even (especially) those reasons you don't agree with.

Miracles

Religion is a great source of stories of <u>weird</u> and <u>wonderful</u> events.

Miracles — when Something Extraordinary Happens

1) Christianity, Islam and Judaism all teach that at some points in history the normal course of events was suspended, and something <u>amazing</u> happened.
2) Some believers, such as some Roman Catholics, think miracles <u>continue</u> to happen up to the <u>present day</u> (e.g. healing at <u>Lourdes</u>) — other Christians believe that we don't live in a time of miracles any more.
3) Others argue that the miracles in religious texts should be interpreted <u>symbolically</u> rather than literally.

The New Testament Contains Many Miracles

The miracle stories are some of the <u>best known</u> of the Bible.

Jesus Controls Nature — Inspiring Awe and Wonder

Jesus performs many <u>miracles</u> in the Gospels. He performs them basically for two reasons — to show that he has <u>God's power</u>, and to demonstrate the importance of <u>faith</u>.

Nothing up my sleeves...

Jesus feeds the 5000 (Mark 6:30-44) A crowd has gathered around Jesus and the disciples, but there are only 5 loaves and 2 fish to eat. Jesus gives thanks to God, and breaks the bread. All 5000 people have enough to eat, and there's enough food left over to fill 12 baskets.

Jesus walks on water (Mark 6:45-52) Jesus catches up with his disciples' boat by walking across the water. Although they have seen him feed the 5000, they are still shocked at his powers.

God has Intervened through Jesus and the Holy Spirit

1) Christians believe that the <u>birth</u>, <u>death</u> and <u>resurrection</u> of Jesus were miracles in their own right (see p.17).
2) At the feast of <u>Pentecost</u> (also known as <u>Whitsun</u>) Christians celebrate the descent of the Holy Spirit on to Jesus's early followers who were instantly able to speak many <u>different languages</u> and were filled with the power to <u>speak out</u> and do <u>amazing things</u> like Jesus did.
3) Many Christians believe that God continues to <u>act</u> in the world <u>today</u> through the Holy Spirit. They believe that the Holy Spirit is the force that <u>guides</u> them to do <u>good</u> in this world.

The Qur'an is a Miracle in Itself

1) Muslims believe the <u>Qur'an</u> is a miracle — the direct word of Allah, with a <u>style</u> that it's <u>impossible</u> to <u>copy</u>.
2) Some Muslims believe that the Qur'an contains 'scientific miracles' — where <u>facts</u> discovered <u>centuries later</u> are described, such as the development of the human embryo (Qur'an 23:12-14). Others argue that the Qur'an is for our <u>spiritual</u> and <u>moral guidance</u>, rather than a source for scientific theories.
3) The Prophet Muhammad didn't work miracles — but many Muslims believe that Allah took him on a <u>journey</u> from <u>Mecca</u> to <u>Jerusalem</u> and on a tour of the heavens in <u>one night</u>. Some Muslims believe it was a <u>spiritual</u> rather than a <u>physical</u> journey. Most Muslims believe that Allah's <u>greatest</u> miracle is <u>creation</u> itself.

Judaism has Plenty of Miracles of its Own

1) There are many <u>miraculous events</u> described in the <u>Hebrew Bible</u>. Examples include G-d parting the <u>Red Sea</u> for Moses during the flight from Egypt (Exodus 14) and the fall of the <u>walls of Jericho</u> (Joshua 6).
2) Some Liberal Jews argue that the purpose of the stories of these miracles is to impart a <u>spiritual message</u>, and they don't have to be believed in literally. More orthodox believers might argue that the events actually occurred as described in scripture.
3) More importantly for Jews, G-d intervened in the world by sending his <u>prophets</u> — such as <u>Isaiah</u> — who they believe <u>represented</u> G-d's will to the Jews. Jews consider <u>Moses</u> the greatest of the prophets.

You won't need a miracle if you learn it all properly...

Although some religious people seek to distance themselves from the belief in miracles, you have to wonder whether their religion would have been so successful without its tales of bizarre and amazing events.

Practice Questions

That's a pretty tricky section to be starting with. But once you've learnt all the facts, had a good think about what you make of it all, and worked out why some people might disagree with you — there's nothing for it but to have a crack at these practice questions.

See how many you can do, then go back through the section and work out answers for those you couldn't do. Then do them again, and again, till you can get through the whole lot. (Don't worry about the questions on religions you're not studying though.)

If you find the longer answer questions tricky, check out the 'Do Well in Your Exam' section towards the back of the book.

1) What is/are:
   a) monotheism?
   b) an agnostic?
   c) omnipotence?
   d) the Trinity? *(Christianity)*
   e) the Nicene Creed? *(Christianity)*
   f) the ninety-nine names? *(Islam)*
   g) a miracle?
   h) the Holy Spirit? *(Christianity)*

These "definition" questions are only worth 1 mark each in the exam, so keep your answers short.

2) a) State two beliefs people have about God/Allah/G-d.
   b) What is meant by a 'design argument' for the existence of a god?
   c) Give two reasons someone may have for believing in a god.
   d) Give two reasons someone might have for believing in miracles.

Don't write an essay for these questions. They're worth 2 marks, so make sure you get two facts down for each of them.

3) a) Describe the questions people have about what God/Allah/G-d is like.
   b) Describe Christian beliefs about the Trinity. *(Christianity)*
   c) Describe how Muslims believe they can come to know Allah. *(Islam)*
   d) Describe what a believer may think about miracles.

These questions are worth up to 3 marks. Make sure you get a good couple of examples down for each question.

4) a) Explain why some believers may not worry about exact definitions for god.
   b) Explain why some believers might be convinced by design arguments.
   c) How might parents encourage their children to believe in a god?
   d) Explain why some people might think believing in miracles is important.

These questions are worth up to 6 marks. Answer them with reference to those religions you're studying.

5) Read the following statements:
   a) "It is not possible to prove God exists."
   b) "God cannot be defined."
   c) "The only reason people have religious faith is because of the way they were brought up."
   d) "Religious people should not believe in miracles."

   Discuss each statement. You should include different, supported points of view and a personal viewpoint. You must refer to a religion in your answer.

These questions are worth 12 marks each, so they're really important. If you're studying Islam and/or Judaism have a go at answering these questions with reference to Allah and/or G-d.

Public and Private Christian Worship

Christianity

Worship is the religious person's way of expressing their <u>love</u> of, <u>respect</u> for, and <u>devotion</u> to a god or gods.

Sunday Worship in Church can take Many Forms

1) Most churches have their main service on a Sunday morning. It may be <u>structured</u> or <u>spontaneous</u>, but virtually all denominations use hymns or songs, Bible readings, and a sermon. The exact form of Sunday worship will <u>vary</u> between denominations.

2) In Roman Catholic, Orthodox, and most Anglican churches it will be <u>structured</u> and <u>liturgical</u> (i.e. it will follow a pattern laid down in writing — with set <u>prayers</u>, and <u>readings</u>).

3) Methodists and other nonconformists have structured but <u>non-liturgical</u> services, e.g. following the '<u>hymn sandwich</u>' pattern, where the service consists of hymns <u>alternating</u> with things like readings, prayers and a sermon.

4) Roman Catholic and Orthodox Sunday services <u>always</u> include <u>Holy Communion</u> (called <u>Mass</u> in the Roman Catholic tradition), and Anglican churches <u>usually</u> do.

5) Pentecostals, House Churches and other independent Christian fellowships may have <u>spontaneous</u>, often <u>charismatic</u> worship (lifting their hands, dancing, etc.).

6) Some Christians hold church services in their own <u>homes</u>. Some because Christianity is <u>prohibited</u> in their country — others as they believe it's more like the simpler worship described in the New Testament.

7) Many Christians worship informally <u>at home</u> (not just on Sundays). This can be anything from saying <u>Grace</u> before a meal to singing <u>worship songs</u> with family and friends.

> There are several reasons for all this variety. Christians <u>share</u> the same <u>basic beliefs</u> about the importance of Holy Communion, the Bible, the sermon, the Holy Spirit etc., but they <u>differ</u> as to which matters <u>most</u>.

Inside A Typical Parish Church

Traditional Roman Catholic and Church of England churches are often very similar in layout:

① ALTAR
The most important place in the church — a table which holds the items for the <u>Communion</u> service. The <u>altar</u> is in the east end.

② EAST WINDOW
Often of <u>stained glass</u>, it's right behind the altar and draws attention to it.

③ PULPIT
A raised box from which the <u>minister</u> gives the <u>sermon</u> or talks to the congregation.

④ REREDOS
Some churches have a <u>painted</u> or sculpted <u>screen</u> behind the altar. It often has pictures of Jesus, Mary or saints, and it helps to focus attention on the altar.

⑤ SANCTUARY
A <u>raised platform</u> where the most <u>important</u> parts of a service take place.

⑦ COVERED FONT
Used to hold <u>water</u> for <u>baptism</u>.

⑥ LECTERN
A stand for the <u>church Bible</u>. Often made from brass and in the shape of an eagle.

⑧ NAVE
The main part of the church where the <u>congregation</u> sits (or originally stood).

⑨ AISLE
Aisles are often used in <u>processions</u>.

There's no sanctuary from revision...

Make sure you spend time learning what each little feature of a church is called and what it's used for.

Christianity

Symbolism in Christian Worship

Symbols are used within the Christian tradition to represent what's believed.
An obvious example is the symbol of the cross — used to represent the sacrificial death of Jesus Christ.

Religious Architecture is often Symbolic

1 Cathedrals can be enormous, demonstrating their importance. They were historically built at the centre of the community to represent God's kingship on Earth. Inside, the focus of attention is always towards the altar, where the main act of worship (the celebration of Holy Communion) takes place.

2 Orthodox churches are often in the shape of a cross, with a large dome on top symbolising Christ's presence, eternity and the nearness of heaven. Inside they are richly decorated with friezes and carvings.

3 Free Churches (e.g. Baptists) meet in simple halls where the pulpit is the focus of attention. This shows the importance to them of preaching from the Bible. Also in a Baptist church, the prominence of the Baptistry (a pool for baptism by total immersion) shows the central importance of baptism.

Icons, Statues and Stained-Glass Windows are Symbolic

1 Icons are paintings (mostly of saints) often found in Orthodox churches, and are often greeted with a kiss on entering the building. They're used to represent the presence of saints, and as a means to pray — 'prayers captured on wood'.

Statues also represent the presence of the saints.

In certain festivals a madonna (a statue of Mary) or another saint is paraded through the streets as an appeal to bless the community.

2 Large cathedrals and churches are often decorated with colourful murals or frescoes, and many feature beautiful stained-glass windows depicting biblical stories.

For centuries the finest work of leading artists was made for churches — all to offer to God the highest expression of worship, and to create a sense of awe.

3 The most well known Christian symbol is the cross which represents Jesus's crucifixion. However a cross isn't a crucifix unless it features a representation of Jesus. Crucifixes can be found in Roman Catholic and Orthodox churches, to remind them of Jesus's suffering — but empty crosses are found in Anglican, Baptist and Methodist churches to remind them of the risen Christ.

4 Another important symbol of Christianity from the earliest times is the fish. Jesus called on his followers to be *"fishers of men"* (Mark 1:17). The Greek word for fish 'ICTHYS' forms an acrostic (each letter becomes the first letter of a new word) for 'Jesus Christ, God's Son, Saviour' in Greek. It was a sign used by early Christians who were being persecuted.

Church Music is also Symbolic

Church music is symbolic as it is used to praise God and to express belief. Mozart, Bach, Beethoven and many other great composers wrote music for worship — e.g. Handel's Messiah, Mozart's Requiem Mass.

1) Hymns have been part of Christian worship for many centuries — they're often derived from passages of scripture.
2) In some Protestant churches, choirs have an important role in leading the singing. There are many types, from Anglican schoolboys to Pentecostal gospel.
3) Many different musical instruments are used in worship — from pipe organs to brass bands and guitars. The music used in worship can be solemn and dignified or loud and lively depending on the type of church.
4) Dancing is common in Charismatic churches — it's seen as a sign of the Holy Spirit's presence.

Who sang that duff note? — hymn...

Don't forget that Christian beliefs are often expressed through worship in ritual form (e.g. baptism), and that this is also a kind of symbolism. Oh, it's all good fun and a whole lot more interesting than maths. So there.

Public and Private Jewish Worship

Judaism

A Jewish place of worship is called a <u>synagogue</u>, although Jews more often use the word '<u>shul</u>', or sometimes even '<u>Bet ha-Knesset</u>' (House of Meeting).

It's not what's on the Outside that matters...

There are <u>no</u> rules stating what a synagogue should look like on the <u>outside</u> — they can be plain or ornate, traditional or ultra modern. But you might recognise a synagogue from <u>symbols</u> on its outside walls, such as a <u>menorah</u> (a seven-branched candlestick), or a <u>magen David</u> (a six-pointed star/shield of David).

...it's what's on the Inside that's Important

The layout of the synagogue's <u>Prayer Hall</u> is based on that of the ancient <u>Temple</u>. It faces <u>Jerusalem</u>, where the Temple stood, and is usually <u>rectangular</u>. All synagogues share the following <u>four features</u>:

1 <u>Aron Kodesh</u> (the <u>Ark</u>) — this is the most important item of furniture, since it holds the Torah. It is a large <u>cupboard</u> or <u>alcove</u>, with doors or a screen, set on the wall facing Jerusalem.

2 <u>Ner Tamid</u> (Perpetual Light) — above the ark is a <u>light</u> which <u>never</u> goes out. It represents the menorah which was always kept alight in the <u>Temple</u>.

> Remember — there will be no 'pictures of God'.

3 <u>Sefer Torah</u> (Scroll of the Torah) — parchment <u>scroll</u>. On each end is a wooden pole for winding it to the required passage. It must be <u>handwritten</u> by a <u>sofer</u> (scribe), and is usually decorated. It's kept inside the ark.

4 <u>Bimah</u> or <u>Almemar</u> — a raised <u>platform</u> with a reading desk, normally in the centre of the hall.

Also, some synagogues have a <u>pulpit</u>, and the <u>Ten Commandments</u> above the ark. Some have an <u>organ</u> (but on the Sabbath, all singing should be <u>unaccompanied</u>), and an Orthodox synagogue will have a <u>gallery</u> where women can sit.

Shabbat (Sabbath) is Celebrated in the Synagogue...

The Sabbath is a day of rest to commemorate the <u>7th Day of Creation</u> when God rested after making the Universe. It begins at <u>sunset</u> on Friday, and ends on Saturday evening when <u>stars</u> begin to appear.

There are 3 separate <u>services</u> in the synagogue on the Sabbath.

> The <u>4th Commandment</u> instructs Jews to observe the Sabbath.
> *"Remember the Sabbath day by keeping it holy."* — Exodus 20:8

FRIDAY EVENING Shabbat is welcomed as a <u>queen</u> or a <u>bride</u> with singing led by a <u>chazan</u> (cantor). No instruments are used — in memory of the destruction of the Temple with its instrumental music.

SATURDAY MORNING the <u>main</u> service of the week. The <u>rabbi</u> will read from the Torah and give a sermon. Also, seven men are called up to read or recite a blessing, and an eighth reads a portion from the books of the Prophets. In Orthodox synagogues, women sit <u>separately</u> from the men and take little part.

> Much like God, I believe in resting on a Saturday.

SATURDAY AFTERNOON this service includes a reading from the <u>Torah</u>, and three special <u>prayers</u>.

Remember the Sabbath — there might be a question on it...

There are big similarities with all three of the faiths covered in this book. Each religion has a day or more a week set aside for special religious observance. Until the mid 1990s most shops in Britain weren't allowed to open on a Sunday. In Israel, government agencies don't open during Shabbat.

Philosophy 1.2 — Religious and Spiritual Experience

Symbolism in Jewish Worship

...and in the Home

1) To prepare for Shabbat, the house is cleaned and tidied, and all the food to be eaten on Shabbat is cooked in advance. Family members bathe or shower. At dusk, the mother of the family will light two candles and welcome the Sabbath by saying a blessing and gesturing with her arms.

2) At the beginning of the Shabbat meal, a sanctifying ceremony called kiddush takes place. It happens at home and at the synagogue, and includes the reciting of Genesis 2:1-3 (God resting after creation). Wine is used to symbolise the sweetness and joy of Shabbat.

> The Mishnah lists 39 kinds of 'work' not allowed on the Sabbath.

3) Challot are eaten — these are two plaited loaves which commemorate the double portion of 'manna' which God provided the day before each Shabbat during the Exodus. They are blessed, cut and dipped in salt.

4) After the father has blessed his children, the Shabbat meal is eaten.

5) The havdalah ('division') ceremony marks the end of Shabbat, separating it from the six days ahead. Blessings are said over sweet-smelling spices, a cup of wine, and over a special plaited candle.

Symbols: Visible Signs of Invisible Ideas...

Since God is invisible, symbols are important in just about every religion. Believers use symbols to help them focus on God in private prayer and in communal worship. A picture on a wall, a household object and an item of clothing may all be used as religious symbols.

But Jews have No Pictures of G-d

There are two reasons why Jewish art never tries to picture G-d.
1) No one knows what he looks like.
2) The 2nd of the 10 Commandments forbids it as idolatry.

> "You shall not make for yourself an idol in the form of anything in heaven above or on the earth beneath..." Exodus 20:4

To avoid idolatry no images of people are allowed in synagogues, as people are made in the image of G-d, The ban on idolatry also means three-dimensional sculptures aren't allowed.
Many synagogues won't have images of animals either, although the 'Lion of Judah' (a symbol of Judaism) can sometimes be found.

Why 'G-d'?

In Deuteronomy (12:1-4) G-d tells the Jews to tear down the temples and wipe out the names of the gods they find written in the sacred places of other nations in Israel. But verse 4 warns them not to do the same to him. Many Jews take this as a warning never to erase the name of G-d — so they never write it out fully just in case.

Symbols in the Home: the Mezuzah

> "These commandments that I give you today are to be upon your hearts... Write them on the doorframes of your houses..." Deuteronomy 6:6-9

1) The mezuzah is a sign which is put in Jewish houses.
2) It's a tiny parchment scroll containing the words of Deuteronomy 6:4-9 and 11:13-21 in Hebrew. It must be handwritten by a trained scribe, and is put inside a case to keep it safe.
3) There's one on the front door and every other door of the house except the bathroom and toilet. It constantly reminds the family of their duty to G-d.

This page must seem like manna from heaven...

Jews also use ritual dress. The kippah is a skullcap, worn as a sign of respect for God. Tefillin are boxes containing four Bible passages, tied to the head and upper arm. These remind Jews to serve God with head and heart (see p13). And the tallit is a prayer shawl, with tassels on each corner, to obey Numbers 15:37-41.

Public and Private Muslim Worship

A mosque (or masjid) is more than a place of worship — it's also a centre of the community for Muslims. Masjid literally means 'place of prostration' (i.e. lying with the face down) — an act of submission to God.

A Mosque (Masjid) is the Muslim House of Prayer

1) The Prophet Muhammad said that any clean place could be used for worship.

2) Some mosques are extremely simple, others are very grand, but all have a dome representing the universe.

3) Most mosques will have at least one minaret. This is a tall tower from where the muezzin (mu'adhin in Arabic) calls the adhan (call to prayer).

Inside the Mosque

"Muhammad"

"Allah"

1) Beautiful mosaic tiles often decorate both the outside and inside of a mosque.

2) There are no pictures of Muhammad or Allah, since no one is allowed to draw them, and pictures of other living things are usually banned, to avoid idolatry.

3) The ban on images means that richly coloured Arabic calligraphy (writing) is often used to decorate mosques with words from the Qur'an and the names of Allah and Muhammad. The faith of the calligrapher is expressed in writing — this helps the believer focus on the meaning of the words. Calligraphy is one of the most respected arts in the Islamic world.

4) Shoes must be left at the door, and every mosque must have somewhere for Muslims to wash before prayer.

5) There are no seats, but the whole floor is usually covered with rich carpet.

6) There is little in the way of furniture, but you will see a pulpit (called a minbar), where the imam (a respected person) will lead prayers from — especially on Fridays.

7) Muslims face Makkah when they pray, and a special niche (called the mihrab) in the 'direction-wall' shows the direction in which Makkah lies.

Apart from prayer, a mosque is used as a Madrasah (a mosque school), where Muslims learn the general principles of Islam, as well as how to carry out Muslim practices and recite the Qur'an.

MEN, WOMEN AND THE MOSQUE

The main service in the mosque is on Friday, and all males are expected to attend unless they're ill or travelling. Women don't have to attend the mosque, but if they do they must pray in a separate group from men. Also, women do not lead prayers in a mosque if a man is available, but they may lead other women and children.

Home life also has an important role in Islam — this is where many of the rules of Islam are kept.
- Most Muslim households have a copy of the Qur'an.
- It's where children first learn and witness Islamic values.
- It is also the centre of religious life for many women, who are not obliged to attend the mosque.

Tawhid is the belief in the Oneness of Allah

1) Islam teaches that nothing is remotely like Allah, and nothing can be compared to him.

2) The worst sin for a Muslim would be to believe that God was not supreme — this concept is called Shirk. (Shirk is the opposite of Tawhid.)

Muslim beliefs about Allah...
Allah is beyond time and space. He is the Almighty One, the Compassionate and the Merciful. All men and women owe their creation, and continued existence, to Allah — the One and Only Creator.

And see page 3 for more basic Muslim beliefs about God.

This all needs to be learnt — you'd better believe it...

...but only if you're studying Islam. If you have a Mosque near you, see if you can find any calligraphy on the walls. Notice how the words are shaped to be more beautiful and to reflect their meanings. Even if you can't read Arabic, the calligraphy is quite a sight.

Prayer and Meditation

Prayer is at the centre of many people's faith. Whereas worship involves all the things people do to express their faith, prayer is specifically the 'talking to God/G-d/Allah' part.

Prayer Puts People In Touch with their God

1) Prayer is when believers mentally or vocally communicate with their god, or gods.
2) Prayer comes in many different forms: most branches of Christianity, Judaism and Islam have set prayers that people say when they are engaged in their main acts of worship.
3) But prayer also has a private dimension where the individual believer communicates with their god in their own words.
4) Some prayers have set words — these include the Lord's Prayer in Christianity and the Shema in Judaism.
5) Some religions require specific movements for some prayers — such as the Muslim Salah prayers (see next page), which require believers to take various positions including prostrating themselves with their hands, knees and foreheads placed on to the ground.

Prayer can be a Powerful Thing

1) There's a strong tradition in Christian prayer of asking for things from God. When believers feel that God grants their requests this is known as an 'answered prayer'. Some believers think answered prayers are proof that God exists.
2) However this presents the problem of 'unanswered prayers' when God doesn't grant a believer's request.
3) Some Christians argue that God answers all prayers in his own way and in his own time. Others would argue that God has bigger plans that we cannot understand — He moves in mysterious ways.
4) Jesus himself on the night of his arrest prays: "My father, if it is possible, may this cup be taken from me. Yet not as I will, but as you will." (Matthew 26:39). The "cup" may represent suffering.
5) Roman Catholics and Orthodox believers pray to saints to ask for their 'intercession' (help) with God. They believe that the Saints can join in our prayers to God, making them more effective.
6) Protestant churches believe that Jesus is the only mediator between us and God, so we don't need the Saints' help. Some argue that we shouldn't pray to Saints, as no-one does in the Bible.

Private Prayer draws a Believer Closer to God

Christian prayer is a conversation with God, and should take place both in church and in private. The whole point of prayer is for the believer to draw close to God to communicate with him and hear what he's saying — this deepens their faith. Different Christians use different methods to accomplish this:

The 'Quiet Time' — time spent alone with God, perhaps reading the Bible and praying.

Meditation — a form of prayer where the believer clears his or her mind of distracting thoughts and concentrates on God's nature or work. It may involve repeating a prayer over and over again.

Contemplation — true Christian contemplation is not merely deep thinking — it's intimate wordless prayer in which the believer senses God's presence strongly.

The Rosary — used by Catholics, this is a string of beads arranged in groups. As the beads are moved through the fingers, prayers are said, e.g. the Lord's Prayer, Ave Maria (Hail Mary) and the Gloria.

Icons — Orthodox Christians use icons (sacred pictures of saints) to help them focus on God. Although they may light a candle in front of the icon or kiss it, they don't pray to it.

Many parents pray with their children, believing this encourages them to grow up as praying Christians. And many Christians believe praying while ill brings God's healing or helps them accept their suffering as part of God's plan.

Your prayers are more likely to be answered if you revised first...

Prayer isn't necessarily as straightforward as you might think. People like monks and nuns can devote a whole lifetime to prayer, and it's something they have to work at. If you go to the religion section in your local bookshop you might find books on learning how to pray. But for your exam, you just need to learn this page.

Prayer and Meditation

The Jewish holy day is the <u>Shabbat</u> (<u>Sabbath</u>), but in Judaism, prayer is important every day of the week.

Jews have Three Special Times for Daily Prayer

1) <u>Prescribed</u> daily prayers happen at three special times — in the <u>morning</u>, <u>afternoon</u> and <u>evening</u>.

2) At these times, <u>men</u> will try to attend the <u>synagogue</u> and become part of a <u>minyan</u> — a group of at least ten men, which is the minimum needed for a service. <u>Women</u> (traditionally because of their domestic commitments) are trusted to pray <u>at home</u>.

3) As well as the normal daily prayers, there are also special prayers for getting up, going to bed, before and after eating... in fact, pretty much <u>every</u> event in life, good or bad, can be a reason to pray.

4) The Jewish prayer book is known as the <u>Siddur</u>, which sets out the time of day for different prayers.

5) When praying, Jewish men will often wear a <u>kippah</u> (a skullcap) — although many Orthodox Jews wear them throughout the day. It reminds them that God's intelligence is vastly higher than ours.

6) Some Jews wear <u>tefillin</u> (or phylacteries) while praying. These are leather boxes that contain passages from scripture that are tied to the head and arm during the morning prayer on weekdays. This fulfils the commandment in Deuteronomy 6:8 — "*Tie them* [the commandments] *as symbols on your hands and bind them on your foreheads.*"

Prayer is a Pillar of Islam

You can't be a Muslim without <u>praying</u> in the way Muhammad did. Regular prayer keeps Allah in a Muslim's mind. It also keeps Muslims aware of their <u>duty</u> to obey Allah.

1) Muslims should pray <u>five times</u> a day — at sunrise, early afternoon, late afternoon, after sunset, and late at night.

2) The <u>muezzin</u> makes the call to prayer (<u>adhan</u>) from the <u>minaret</u> of a <u>mosque</u>. The call to prayer begins *"Allahu Akbar..."* (*God is Greatest*).

3) Ideally prayer should take place in a <u>mosque</u>. If this isn't possible, a <u>prayer mat</u> should be used to make a prayer place.

4) <u>Wudu</u> (washing exposed parts of the body three times before prayer) is important, so that a Muslim is <u>pure</u> and <u>clean</u> when approaching Allah.

5) A Muslim should face <u>Makkah</u> (Muhammad's place of birth) when praying. The direction of Makkah is called the <u>qiblah</u>. A compass can be used to find the qiblah (which in England is roughly southeast).

6) There is a set <u>ritual</u> for prayer — each unit of prayer is known as a <u>rak'ah</u> (and the rak'ah may be repeated <u>several</u> times at each prayer session). Each rak'ah involves <u>standing</u>, then <u>kneeling</u>, then putting your <u>forehead</u> to the ground as a sign of submission.

7) If several Muslims are praying in one place, then they all do the ritual <u>together</u> as a sign of <u>unity</u>.

8) <u>Friday</u> prayers are called <u>Salat-al-Jum'ah</u> (or just <u>Jum'ah</u>) — it's a community occasion, and at least 40 people should be there, all praying together.

Women and men pray separately — so people keep their mind on Allah rather than on the opposite sex.

Salah is <u>compulsory</u> prayer. Extra prayers are called <u>du'a</u>, and Muslims can do these at <u>any time</u>. In Du'a prayers, <u>beads</u> can be used — 99 beads for the 99 names of Allah.

Benefits of Prayer
1) Keeps you in close <u>contact</u> with Allah and stops you <u>forgetting</u> him.
2) Expression of <u>solidarity</u> — doing exactly the <u>same</u> as all other Muslims.
3) Moral and spiritual <u>discipline</u>.

Problems with Praying in 'non-Muslim' countries

In <u>non-Muslim</u> countries it can often be hard to pray at the right time, e.g. when you have to go to <u>school</u> or <u>work</u>. This is one of the ways in which life is more <u>complicated</u> for Muslims if they live in a country where Islam is <u>not</u> the way of life of most people.

Five a day — it's not just fruit...

You can see why religion is such a big part of the lives of Jews and Muslims when they have to pray however many times a day. I guess that's one of the main points of prayer — keeping your god in your mind throughout the day. Just don't forget — it's three times for Jews (on ordinary weekdays) and five times for Muslims.

Food and Fasting

Even religious people have got to eat. But not all the time...

Food is Important in Many Religions

1) One of the main ways in which cultures (religious or not) express themselves is through food. This is especially true at special times of year — i.e. during festivals.

2) Christians, Muslims and Jews all believe that God is the creator, and so ultimately, all food comes from Him.

3) Permanent prohibitions (bans) of certain foods are a common feature of many religions, although Christianity is an exception. Most cultures avoid certain food that others may eat anyway, e.g. frogs' legs or dog meat.

4) Fasting (not eating for a period of time) is a part of many religions either as atonement (see below), or as a way to focus the mind on spiritual matters.

Fasting — Not Vital in Christianity

1) Christians believe fasting can help you draw closer to God, but there are no longer any compulsory fasts for Christians, or special foods they must eat or avoid. However Roman Catholics shouldn't eat meat on Ash Wednesday and Good Friday, and they should fast for an hour before the Eucharist (Holy Communion).

2) Lent (February/March) celebrates the 40 days and nights of Jesus' fasting in the wilderness after his baptism. Few Christians today fast during Lent, but many still give up certain luxuries. Lent ends on the day before Easter.

3) Festival foods (e.g. Christmas pudding, hot-cross buns) tend to be more cultural than religious in origin.

- The day before Lent begins is called Shrove Tuesday, a day for being 'shriven' (absolved from sin). Rich foods should be eaten up. Mardi Gras carnivals may be held ('carnival' means 'farewell to meat'). In some countries, like the UK, many people still eat pancakes on Shrove Tuesday — Pancake Day.
- Whether religious or not, many people celebrate Easter (March/April) with Easter eggs, whether with hard-boiled and decorated versions of the real thing, or with chocolate versions, as a symbol of new life.
- Historically Christian countries often have special meals for Christmas (although some countries eat them on Christmas eve). In the UK 'Christmas Dinner' usually consists of roast turkey with stuffing and then Christmas pudding.

4) Don't forget that most Christian denominations celebrate the Eucharist (or Mass or Holy Communion) with bread (usually a communion wafer) and wine. This food and drink represents (and in some denominations is believed to become) the body and blood of Christ.

Kashrut — the Jewish Food Laws

1) Observant Orthodox Jews follow a special diet based on the Kashrut (Jewish food laws).

2) Permitted food is called kosher — everything else is terefah ('torn').

3) These laws are an example of statutes laid down by G-d to test Jews' obedience, and to mark them out as different from other nations.

4) To be kosher, a mammal must have cloven (split) hooves and chew the cud. Fish with fins and scales are kosher, but no other seafood is. Some birds are also kosher.

5) Animals and birds must be specially slaughtered with one cut across the throat using a razor-sharp blade. Blood must not be eaten, and meat and dairy products must not be eaten together. Foods that aren't meat or dairy may be eaten with either.

In Judaism, food is associated with happiness — so fasting shows grief or repentance.

Judaism teaches that true repentance can atone (i.e. make amends) for any past transgression — 'the gates of repentance are always open'.

Which religion is it that gets the burgers?

Eating is something everyone has to do — so it's no wonder that it pops up as a topic in pretty much every religion. Many non-religious families make a point of getting together for a big family meal as often as possible. But religious people have lots of special foods and fasts — and you've got to learn 'em all.

Food and Fasting

Jews Fast for Some Festivals...

1) <u>Yom Kippur</u> (the Day of Atonement) is the most important <u>fast</u> in the Jewish calendar. Taking place ten days after the start of the Jewish New Year (Rosh Hashanah), it involves prayer and fasting for 25 hours from half an hour before nightfall on the eve of Yom Kippur, through to half an hour after nightfall on Yom Kippur itself.

2) Not only do Jews refrain from eating during Yom Kippur, they also don't <u>drink</u> — not even water. Yom Kippur is the day when Jews ask G-d to forgive the sins they committed over the past year. They abstain from food and drink the better to focus on <u>spiritual</u> rather than physical matters.

...and Eat Special Food at Others

1) One of the most important Jewish feasts of the year is <u>Pesach</u> (<u>Passover</u>). It commemorates the night before the <u>Exodus</u> — when <u>Moses</u> led the Israelite slaves from Egypt to freedom. In Egypt, the angel of death killed the first-born sons of the Egyptians, but <u>passed over</u> the Israelites.

2) <u>Yeast</u> is forbidden — all bread must be <u>unleavened</u>. The <u>Seder</u> (Passover meal) involves the symbolic arrangement and eating and drinking of matzah (a cracker-like unleavened bread), wine, salt water, bitter herbs, karpas (a vegetable), roast or hard-boiled egg, and a roasted lamb bone which isn't eaten.

3) During the <u>Shavuot</u> festival in early summer, Jews traditionally eat dairy products like cheesecake.

4) For <u>Hanukkah</u>, a wintertime festival, Jews traditionally eat fried foods like latkes (potato pancakes) and doughnuts, to celebrate the story of a day's worth of oil burning for eight days during the rededication ceremony for the Temple in Jerusalem.

Muslims Fast During Ramadan

1) Muslims must <u>fast</u> between <u>sunrise</u> and <u>sunset</u> during the month of <u>Ramadan</u> in the Muslim calendar.

2) This fasting means no <u>food</u>, no <u>drink</u>, no <u>smoking</u> and no <u>sex</u>. Ramadan is a time of both physical and moral <u>self-discipline</u>, and a time of <u>total</u> obedience to Allah.

3) It's supposed to help Muslims <u>understand</u> hunger, and so makes them more <u>willing</u> to help others.

4) It's also a time to show publicly that Allah matters more than <u>physical</u> needs.

5) <u>Sawm</u> (fasting during Ramadan) is one of the most important obligations for a Muslim.

6) <u>Eid ul-Fitr</u> marks the end of Ramadan. There are special prayers, and Muslims enjoy <u>rich meals</u> with their families.

> There are <u>exceptions</u> to the normal Ramadan rules:
> 1) <u>Children</u> don't have to fast until they're about 12 years old.
> 2) People can be excused for <u>medical</u> reasons. Those who are <u>ill</u> (and women having their <u>period</u>) are excused. And it's okay to take <u>medicine</u> which has to be regular, e.g. antibiotics.
> 3) If you're on a <u>journey</u>, you can be excused. But you have to <u>make up</u> the missed days later.

7) <u>Eid ul-Adha</u> is the <u>festival of sacrifice</u>. It commemorates <u>Ibrahim's</u> willingness to sacrifice his son to Allah. Sheep and goats are sacrificed at the festival, and the meat is <u>shared</u> among the poor.

The Shari'ah says things are either Halal or Haram

HALAL means 'allowed'	HARAM means 'forbidden'

You need to know these two Arabic words. Think of the letter L — ha**L**a**L** is a**LL**owed. And HA**R**a**M** can <u>HARM</u>.

Food Laws — No Pork, No Blood at all, No animals that Eat Meat

1) The basic rules are <u>no pork</u>, <u>no blood</u> at all, and <u>no animals that eat meat</u>.

2) This means it's very important how an animal is killed — it must be done by slitting the neck and allowing all the blood to drain out. Meat from animals killed like this is halal, i.e. allowed.

3) Food <u>preparation</u> is also important — <u>no animal fat</u> can be used (but vegetable oil is okay).

4) <u>Intoxicants</u>, e.g. alcohol, are also forbidden.

What, no chips?

Remember, some fasts are for a whole day, whereas other fasts last longer, but only during daylight hours.

Practice Questions

Religious and Spiritual Experience — I guess that's getting right down to what being a religious believer is all about. Here's another set of questions for you to get your teeth into. Make sure you answer them for all of the religions you're studying.

1) What is/are:

   a) a religious symbol?

   b) an icon? *(Christianity)*

   c) a menorah? *(Judaism)*

   d) a Madrasah? *(Islam)*

   e) tawhid? *(Islam)*

   f) prayer?

   g) the Rosary? *(Christianity)*

   h) the Siddur? *(Judaism)*

   i) wudu? *(Islam)*

   j) fasting?

   k) Lent? *(Christianity)*

   l) Sawm? *(Islam)*

The glossary at the end of this book is pretty handy for revising for these 1 mark questions.

2) a) What is meant by 'worship'?

   b) Name two features of a church/mosque/synagogue.

   c) Describe two ways in which churches/mosques/synagogues use symbolism.

   d) State two things a Christian/Muslim/Jew might believe about prayer.

   e) What is meant by 'halal'/'kosher' food? *(Islam) (Judaism)*

These questions are just about knowing the basic facts of the religions you're studying. They're only worth 2 marks each.

3) a) What is the difference between liturgical and non-liturgical worship? *(Christianity)*

   b) How might a Jew observe the Shabbat? *(Judaism)*

   c) How do Christians/Muslims/Jews pray?

   d) Describe Christian/Muslim/Jewish beliefs about fasting.

   e) How do Christians/Muslims/Jews celebrate a special occasion with food?

Make sure you back up your answers to these 3-mark questions with facts. If you can use the specialist vocabulary you've learnt, even better.

4) a) Explain why some Christians do not pray to the Saints. *(Christianity)*

   b) Explain why some Christian churches are decorated with images. *(Christianity)*

   c) Explain why there are no pictures of Allah/G-d in mosques/synagogues. *(Islam) (Judaism)*

   d) Explain why some Muslims may be excused from fasting. *(Islam)*

Read these questions carefully, or you may end up giving reasons why people do something when you're supposed to give reasons why they don't. That's an easy way to throw away 6 marks.

5) Read the following statements:

   a) "It should not matter to Christians what their church looks like." *(Christianity)*

   b) "Symbolism is very important to religious people."

   c) "Unanswered prayers prove that there is no god."

   d) "It doesn't matter what religious people eat."

Discuss each statement. You should include different, supported points of view and a personal viewpoint. You must refer to a religion in your answer.

You need to use good spelling, grammar and punctuation for these questions. Write your answer in proper sentences. Each one's worth 12 marks in the exam.

Life After Death: Christianity

Every religion in the world has got something to say about death — and what they say can have quite an effect. What people believe will happen to them in <u>death</u> can influence the way they <u>live</u> their lives.

Life After Death — *Some People Believe, Others Don't*

1) Some people believe that when you die, that's it — your body decays and you <u>cease to exist</u>.

2) Others believe that, although your <u>body</u> may die and decay, your <u>soul</u> can live on — in other words, you move on to a different kind of existence. This is the basic idea of <u>life after death</u>.

3) Most religions have a concept of <u>soul</u> — that part of a human being that isn't part of the physical world. Most religions believe something happens to this soul after death. Some religions teach that the soul is <u>rewarded</u> or <u>punished</u> for the actions of the person on Earth. Others teach that the soul is placed into another body for another life (reincarnation).

4) Even some <u>non-religious</u> people believe in souls. The big differences between those things that are alive (like us) and those that aren't (like rocks) suggests to some people that there might be something special inside us that isn't just more stuff.

5) The fact that people are <u>conscious</u> (aware) of themselves in a way that even other animals aren't is taken by many to suggest that this awareness must be separate from everyday matter.

Christian Teaching — *Heaven and Hell*

1) Christianity teaches that the <u>soul</u> lives on after death (<u>immortality</u> of the soul), and that the body will be <u>resurrected</u> (brought back to life) for Judgement Day, just as Jesus was resurrected after his crucifixion.

2) Christians believe that God will judge you, and you'll go either to <u>Heaven</u>, or to <u>Hell</u>:

   • Heaven is often portrayed as a place of great beauty and serenity, a <u>paradise</u> where you'll spend eternity with God — as long as you believe in <u>Jesus Christ</u>, have followed his teachings and have lived a <u>good</u> life, that is. Those in Heaven are said to belong to the <u>Communion of Saints</u>.

   • Hell, on the other hand, is portrayed as a place of <u>torment</u> and <u>pain</u> — the final destination of <u>nonbelievers</u> and those who have led <u>bad</u> lives.

And in Hell they make you wear bad wigs and false moustaches... <u>forever.</u>

3) However, not all Christians believe that these are <u>real</u> places — many Christians see Heaven and Hell as <u>states of mind</u>. In Heaven you'll be <u>happy</u>, and know God — in Hell you'll be <u>unable</u> to know God's love.

4) A few believe that those who God finds unacceptable will be <u>annihilated</u>. They had no interest in spiritual things when they were <u>alive</u>, therefore their spirits were never awakened and cannot survive death.

5) Roman Catholics also believe in a place, or state of existence, called <u>Purgatory</u>. Here <u>sins</u> are punished before the soul is able to move on to Heaven. This concept isn't in the Bible, so Protestants reject it.

6) The fear of punishment or promise of rewards in the afterlife <u>encourages</u> believers to live <u>good lives</u>. But many Christians believe even those who led sinful lives may find <u>salvation</u> thanks to God's saving power.

"Whoever lives and believes in me will never die"

This is how the Christian Church sees death and resurrection:

1) Human beings <u>sin</u>, meaning that they don't live up to God's perfect standard. Because of this, they're not <u>fit</u> to be accepted into Heaven.

2) But Jesus <u>redeemed</u> his followers by <u>sacrificing</u> himself to pay for our sins. He <u>broke</u> the power of sin and death — his power and goodness were so <u>great</u> that after he was crucified, death couldn't keep hold of him. Jesus promised that, just as he had been <u>saved</u> from death, anyone who <u>followed</u> him would find salvation.

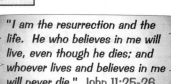

"I am the resurrection and the life. He who believes in me will live, even though he dies; and whoever lives and believes in me will never die." John 11:25-26

I've got soul — and I'm super bad...

...said the twentieth-century theologian Mr James Brown. Even if you don't believe in a religion, you can see how belief in an immortal soul affects how people live their lives. If you believed that your life would be judged on how you'd used it, chances are you'd think about your actions in a different way.

Judaism

Life After Death: Judaism

It should come as no surprise at all to learn that Judaism has something to say about <u>death</u> as well.

Sheol — the Shadowy Destination of the Dead

1) Jewish teachings are largely concerned with the <u>earthly</u> life, and a person's <u>duties</u> to God and other people. According to the Torah, rewards for obeying God and punishments for 'breaking the covenant' are sent in <u>this world</u> (Leviticus 26:3-17). But Jews still have a firm belief in the <u>immortality of the soul</u>.

2) When the earliest Jewish scriptures were written, it was believed that after death <u>all souls</u> went to a place called <u>Sheol</u> — where the dead lived as shadows. Sheol was believed to be dark and cold, and your soul would stay there for <u>eternity</u>. This <u>wasn't</u> as a punishment — it's just what was believed to happen.

3) However, over time the Jews came to believe in the <u>resurrection</u> of the dead...

In the Messianic Age the Dead Will be Resurrected

1) Jews believe that the <u>Messiah</u>, a great future leader, will bring an era of <u>perfect peace</u> and <u>prosperity</u> called the <u>World to Come</u> (or <u>messianic age</u>). (Jews don't believe Jesus was the Messiah.)

> "Multitudes who sleep in the dust of the earth will awake: some to <u>everlasting life</u>, others to shame and <u>everlasting contempt</u>." Daniel 12:2.

2) It's believed that the <u>righteous</u> dead (both Jews and non-Jews) will be <u>resurrected</u> to share in the messianic peace. But the <u>wicked</u> dead won't be resurrected — they gave up their share in the World to Come by living sinful lives.

3) Orthodox Jews believe that the <u>physical body</u> will be resurrected, <u>intact</u>, in the messianic age. Because of this, the body shouldn't be cut after death (<u>autopsies</u> are frowned upon) and cremation is <u>forbidden</u>. A Jewish cemetery is called the '<u>House of Life</u>' (Bet ha-Chaim), which reaffirms the view that the body will be resurrected.

Okay, it was wrong. But everlasting contempt seems a bit over the top.

4) Reform Jews believe that the body is simply a <u>vessel</u> for the soul, and <u>reject</u> the idea of physical resurrection. So Reform Jews accept cremation and organ donation.

Modern Judaism Teaches of Gan Eden and Gehinnom

1) Modern Jews believe in an afterlife spent in places called <u>Gan Eden</u> ("Garden of Eden" or Paradise) and <u>Gehinnom</u> (a bit like Purgatory), but they don't tend to have firm beliefs on the <u>specifics</u> of the afterlife.

2) Some see Gan Eden as a <u>physical</u> place of lavish banquets and warm sunshine. But others have a more <u>spiritual</u> view of it — as a <u>closeness</u> to God. Similarly, there are different views of Gehinnom — a place of fire and physical <u>torment</u>, or a chance to see <u>missed opportunities</u> and the <u>harm</u> a person caused in life.

3) Only if you've lived a <u>blameless</u> life will you be sent straight to Gan Eden when you die.

4) Most souls are sent to Gehinnom for a period of <u>punishment</u> and <u>purification</u> first, which lasts no longer than <u>12 months</u>, before ascending to Gan Eden. Only the <u>truly wicked</u> never reach Paradise, but there are various ideas about what happens to them, e.g. they're annihilated, or they stay in Gehinnom forever.

Your Behaviour During Your Life is Judged

1) Many Jews believe that your <u>behaviour</u> here will determine what kind of <u>afterlife</u> you receive. This means that there's a strong emphasis on <u>moral behaviour</u> in this life — doing what is <u>right</u> even if it isn't easy or profitable for you.

2) However, some Jews would argue that being virtuous is its own <u>reward</u> — you should do good things simply because they are <u>good</u>.

Will there be exams in the next life?

Of the three religions in this book, Judaism has the least clear ideas about the afterlife. In some ways that makes it harder to learn — you have to know more points of view. But it gives you plenty to write about.

Life After Death: Islam

Islam

Islam has very <u>definite teachings</u> when it comes to life after death.

The Soul is the Real Person

It's <u>free will</u> that makes human beings different from <u>angels</u> — angels obey him <u>perfectly</u>.

1) Muslims believe human beings are Allah's <u>greatest</u> physical creation. They also believe that humans are different from other animals, because we know we will <u>die</u>.

2) Islam teaches that every <u>soul</u> (<u>ruh</u>) is unique and has <u>free will</u>.

Muslims believe in predestination — Al-Qadr. Although we have free will, Islam teaches we cannot do everything we want — God is still in control. In recognition of this, Muslims will often say "insh' Allah" (if God is willing).

3) It is the soul that will be <u>judged</u> after death, as it is the soul that is our <u>consciousness</u>. Our body is thought of as a kind of 'vehicle for the soul'.

4) Muslims call life after death <u>akhirah</u> — it's one of the key Islamic beliefs. Not to have a belief in life after death would make <u>this</u> life meaningless for a Muslim.

5) Islam teaches that nothing that happens to us during our earthly lives is <u>accidental</u> — Muslims believe we are being <u>tested</u>, and that the way we act in life will determine what happens to us after we die.

6) A key teaching of Islam is that we remain in the grave after death in a state called the '<u>cold sleep</u>' until the <u>Day of Judgement</u>. On this day, Allah will judge <u>everyone</u> — not just Muslims.

The Soul Goes to al'Jannah (Paradise) or Jahannam (Hell)

1) Although the <u>earthly</u> life is short compared with the eternal, Muslims believe it's still very important. It's in this life that Allah <u>tests</u> us. On <u>Judgement Day</u>, it's <u>too late</u> to beg forgiveness for any wrongdoing.

2) Islam teaches we are judged on:
   i) our <u>character</u>, ii) our <u>reactions</u> to good and bad events in our lives, iii) our <u>way of life</u>.

3) Muslims believe everything is the <u>will of Allah</u> — so there's no point <u>moaning</u> about your circumstances. We cannot know <u>why</u> things happen, or what Allah wishes us to learn from it. The important thing is that we react to it the <u>right</u> way.

4) The reward for those who have followed Allah will be entry into <u>al'Jannah</u> (<u>Paradise</u>) — this is a place of peace, happiness and beauty. In fact, the Qur'an refers to al'Jannah as '<u>gardens of delight</u>', filled with flowers and birdsong.

5) For those who don't <u>believe</u> in Allah, or have committed bad deeds, the reward is <u>Jahannam</u> (or <u>Hell</u>). The Qur'an describes Jahannam as a place of scorching <u>fire</u>, hot <u>winds</u> and black <u>smoke</u>. Here, those who have ignored Allah's teaching and failed to act righteously will be <u>punished</u> for eternity.

Allah is merciful and compassionate, but at the same time, he's a tough judge. Basically, if you're a good Muslim, you'll go to Paradise. But if you're a bad Muslim or a non-Muslim, you deserve Hell, but you might get lucky and be sent by Allah to Paradise if he's feeling merciful.

6) But Allah is also <u>merciful</u>, so many of those who have lived <u>sinful</u> lives may not be sent to Jahannam.

Being Obedient to Allah is Vital for a Muslim

'<u>Islam</u>' literally means '<u>submission</u>' or '<u>obedience</u>' to Allah. And there are certain day-to-day rules that Allah expects you to follow if you want to <u>show</u> that you're being obedient. The key to getting to Paradise for a Muslim is <u>obedience</u>. The reasoning is as follows...

1) Allah <u>expects</u> obedience, and obedience is a Muslim's <u>duty</u>.
2) If a Muslim does his or her duty, that person will <u>please</u> Allah.
3) If a person pleases Allah enough, they will be sent to <u>Paradise</u> after they die.
4) And if Allah is <u>not</u> pleased with someone, they will be <u>punished</u> after they die.

So this is <u>vital</u> stuff. How a Muslim lives in <u>this</u> life will determine where he or she ends up in the <u>next</u> life.

Stop moaning about your Exam — it is the will of Allah...

Yep, it's true. Don't be put off by the long and difficult words on this page — just get learning and your RS exam will fly by. Don't worry, there's only another three pages to go in this unit...

General & Christianity

Christian Funeral Rites

Every religion has a special way of dealing with the dead.

Funerals are a Way to Say Goodbye

1) While many people never get Christened or have a Bar Mitzvah, nearly everyone gets a funeral.

2) Going back through history, people have always made special provision for their dead — e.g. by mummifying them, burying them, cremating (burning) them or with other rituals, e.g. burial at sea.

3) While UK law only specifies that the body has to be properly disposed of (e.g. buried, cremated) most people, with a religious faith or without, will hold some kind of ceremony.

4) Funerals are seen as a chance to say goodbye to the dead, and to remember and celebrate their lives.

5) Most funerals in Britain are organised by professionals known as funeral directors or undertakers.

6) Mourning is a deep sorrow for someone who has died. Many societies have a period of mourning after a funeral, when loved ones say special prayers for the deceased, remember their lives and forgo pleasures (e.g. music, bright colours, sex). At the end of that period, mourners try to move on with their lives.

Christian Funerals are Sad, but with a Note of Hope

Funeral services vary according to denomination, but all Christian funerals contain a note of hope.
For many this doesn't mean wishful thinking — it means confident expectation based on God's promises.

1) The coffin is carried into the church, and the verses on page 17 from John 11 are often read. There are hymns, other Bible readings and prayers. The priest (or someone else) often gives a short sermon about Christian belief in life after death, and may also talk about the life of the person who has died.

2) Of course there will be sadness too, particularly if the person died young or very suddenly. There are prayers for the bereaved, and members of the congregation will express their sympathy for the family and close friends of the deceased. Black clothes are often worn, though some Christians consider this inappropriate and may even request guests not to dress in this way.

3) It doesn't matter whether the body's buried or cremated — Christians believe that at the Resurrection they will have new 'spiritual bodies', not their old ones. There's another short service at the graveside or crematorium, then afterwards often a meal for family and friends.

> ### Roman Catholic Requiem Mass
> A Roman Catholic funeral includes Holy Communion (the 'Requiem Mass'). The purpose of a Requiem Mass is to pray for the soul of the dead person. The priest wears white vestments, and the coffin is covered with a white cloth (a pall). The coffin is sprinkled with holy water and the priest says, "In the waters of baptism (name) died with Christ, and rose with him to new life. May s/he now share with him in eternal glory." The coffin is later sprinkled again, and also perfumed with incense.

Funeral Customs help Support the Bereaved

1) Christian funeral services have a great deal to say about the hope of eternal life. The bereaved person is encouraged to believe that one day she or he will be reunited with the deceased.

2) In the days following the funeral, family and friends often try to contact those who were closest to the deceased, and encourage them to talk through their grief.

Hmm... Perhaps a bit premature...

3) Usually the priest or vicar will also try to visit, and may offer counselling, or suggest someone who can. There are several stages to the process of grief, and it can help to talk to someone who understands this.

It's not all bad news...

Funerals — cheery subject. But Christians try not to see death as depressing — after all, they believe the person who died is going to Heaven (probably), which has to be a good thing, if you're a Christian. Of course, it'd be a bit of a downer if you thought they might go to Hell, but let's not dwell on that.

Muslim and Jewish Funeral Rites

Muslims and Jews also have rituals surrounding death.

'Allah' should be the Last Word a Muslim Hears

A Muslim hopes not to die alone, but with relatives and friends around, who will:

i) Keep them company and look after them.

ii) Ensure last-minute business is settled, so the dying one is not distracted by things to do with this life.

iii) Pray, and recite 'There is no God but Allah,' so that the person may be helped to concentrate on the name of God. Ideally, just as the name of Allah was the first thing the Muslim heard at birth, it should also be the last at death.

Bodies are Buried Facing Makkah

1) After a person has died, the body is washed, as a sign of respect.

2) The body is then wrapped in a clean white shroud.

3) Funeral prayers (Janazah prayers) are said, praying that the dead person may be judged mercifully and gain a place in Paradise.

4) The body is buried in a simple grave, lying on its right side with the face towards Makkah.

5) A period of mourning is kept for three days, finishing with Qur'an reading and prayers for the dead person. Some Muslims do this after 40 days as well.

> It's said that graves are visited by two angels to question the deceased and work out whether they're fit for the next life.

Judaism has Customs to Comfort the Bereaved

There are many rituals in Judaism concerned with death. They're designed to help bereaved people accept what has happened, give expression to their grief, receive comfort, and come to terms with their loss.

1) Jewish families gather together to be near a loved one who is dying, while the dying person should spend his/her last moments confessing sins and reciting the Shema (see page 2).

2) After the death, each member of an Orthodox family will make a small tear in their clothing — a symbol of grief and shock. This is less common in Reform Judaism.

3) The dead person must not be left alone, and must be buried (not cremated) as soon as possible, preferably within 24 hours. Reform Jews often allow longer, so that the family has more time to organise the funeral.

4) The body is ritually bathed and wrapped in a plain linen shroud, before being placed in a plain, unpolished, wooden coffin — in death rich and poor are equal. This is done by a Chevra Kaddisha (burial society).

5) At the funeral service in the synagogue, psalms are read and a prayer is said praising God for giving life and for taking it away. The rabbi might make a short speech about the deceased.

Mourning Continues for Thirty Days After Death

1) The first week after the funeral is called shiva (seven). The immediate family stay at home and are visited by relatives and friends who pray with them three times a day and offer comfort. They do not cut their hair, shave, listen to music or have sex. The men recite a prayer called the kaddish. Everyone is encouraged to talk about the person who has died.

2) The first month after the funeral is called sheloshim (thirty). During this time life returns gradually to normal, and male mourners go to the synagogue to recite the kaddish. Anyone who has lost a parent remains in mourning for a whole year.

3) The anniversary of death is called yahrzeit. It is usually on the first yahrzeit that the headstone is erected above the grave. Every year a candle is lit for 24 hours and men say the kaddish.

Make sure you get this rite in the exam...

Remember that funeral rites and ideas about the afterlife have a big impact on the living. They not only help people come to terms with the loss of loved ones, but also give plenty to think about for their own lives — Am I living a moral life? Am I going to make it to paradise? How do I want to be remembered?

Practice Questions

Ah... you can't expect to get through a Philosophy unit without a bit of death. But then, the gist seems to be if you've followed your religion, and weren't too naughty, you'll go to heaven (or something akin). What's not to like?
Have a go at these questions. If there are any you can't answer, have another look through the section and then try again. Keep going till you can do them all with your eyes closed and one arm tied to a lamppost. Well, go on...

1) What is:
   a) death?
   b) life after death?
   c) resurrection?
   d) bereavement?
   e) a funeral?
   f) cremation?
   g) mourning?

   These questions get you 1 mark each — so keep your answers short and snappy.

2) a) What is meant by 'immortality of the soul'?
   b) What is meant by 'free will'?
   c) State two things that Christians/Muslims/Jews believe about Heaven/Paradise?
   d) State two things that Christians/Muslims/Jews believe about Hell.

   These questions are worth 2 marks each. Make sure you've learnt all the important terms in the glossary and all the basic facts for the religions you're studying.

3) a) What do Christians/Muslims/Jews believe about the final judgement?
   b) What do Christians/Muslims/Jews believe should be done with the bodies of the dead?
   c) Describe what happens at a Christian/Muslim/Jewish funeral.

   These are worth 3 marks each. Don't worry too much about connecting your points for this question — just get the facts down

4) a) How might a Christian's/Muslim's/Jew's belief in the afterlife affect how they live?
   b) Why do Christians/Muslims/Jews believe that people have souls?
   c) How are Christian/Muslim/Jewish funeral rites designed to comfort the bereaved?
   d) Explain how beliefs about the afterlife may affect how the body is treated after death.

   These are worth 6 marks. Make sure you write properly-structured answers for these questions and the next ones.

5) Read the following statements:
   a) "Only Christians/Muslims/Jews will enjoy eternal life."
   b) "We should worry more about what happens in this world than the next."
   c) "It does not matter what happens to someone's body after death."
   d) "Funerals are more for the living than the dead."

   Discuss each statement. You should include different, supported points of view and a personal viewpoint. You must refer to a religion in your answer.

   These questions are worth 12 marks — so you should be spending about as much time on these as the rest of the questions put together.

Good and Evil

Christianity, Islam & Judaism

All religions have similar basic concepts of <u>good</u> and <u>evil</u>. Evil is anything that's deeply <u>immoral</u>, <u>wrong</u> or <u>harmful</u>. And sadly, there's <u>plenty</u> of it in the world — people suffer from <u>terrible illnesses</u> and die in <u>pain</u>. Some people commit horrible <u>crimes</u> and other people <u>suffer</u> as a result.

The Christian View — Adam & Eve, Satan, a Test of Faith...

1) <u>Christianity</u> and <u>Judaism</u> teach that evil <u>entered</u> the world as a result of <u>Adam and Eve</u> giving in to <u>temptation</u> in the Garden of Eden — this switch from a perfect world to one containing evil is known as '<u>The Fall</u>'.

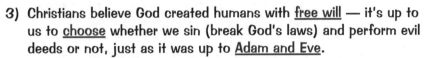

oops...

2) Traditionally, Christianity teaches that every human being was born with a <u>flawed</u> nature after the Fall — this is the idea of <u>original sin</u>. It's believed that this <u>excludes</u> us from Heaven unless we're <u>reconciled</u> with God.
(Not all Christians hold to this any more though — some see the Fall as <u>allegorical</u>.)

Christians believe <u>Jesus</u> was put on Earth to <u>pay</u> for the sins of <u>all humankind</u>. Christianity teaches that the only way we can be forgiven by, and reconciled with, God is through the <u>sacrifice of Jesus</u>. This concept is known as <u>redemption</u>.

3) Christians believe God created humans with <u>free will</u> — it's up to us to <u>choose</u> whether we sin (break God's laws) and perform evil deeds or not, just as it was up to <u>Adam and Eve</u>.

4) Christianity has also <u>personified</u> evil as <u>Satan</u> or the <u>Devil</u> — a <u>supernatural</u> evil force over which we have no control. E.g. in St Paul's letter to the Ephesians, he says:

"Put on the full armour of God so that you can take your stand against the Devil's schemes." Ephesians 6:11

5) Christians might refer to someone who has performed evil deeds as being <u>possessed by the Devil</u>, although this isn't really a part of <u>modern</u> Christian teaching.

6) In Christianity, there are '<u>sins of thought</u>' as well as 'sins of action'. In the Sermon on the Mount, Jesus taught that <u>anger</u> and <u>lustful thoughts</u> are as sinful as murder and adultery (Matthew 5:21-30).

Observing the Mitzvot Keeps Jews from Sinning

1) <u>Modern Judaism</u> has <u>no concept</u> of a <u>devil fighting against</u> <u>G-d</u> and tempting people into doing evil deeds. It is believed that <u>G-d created all</u> — and that includes <u>both good and evil</u>.

<u>Satan</u> is mentioned in the Hebrew Bible (particularly in the <u>Book of Job</u>), but this concept isn't really a part of <u>modern</u> Judaism.

2) Judaism <u>rejects</u> the idea that people are born with sin — they believe that all people are created <u>innocent</u> and only fall into sin later.

3) The Jews define sin as those <u>actions</u> which <u>break the rules</u> (<u>mitzvot</u>) G-d has given them. Just <u>thinking</u> bad things isn't a sin — it's only sinful if you <u>act</u> on those thoughts. Jews believe people have within them an <u>inclination</u> to do bad things, but G-d's rules give them a method for <u>controlling</u> those urges.

Muslims Believe in Iblis — the Shaytan

1) Muslims believe that Adam and Eve sinned only for <u>themselves</u>, and that they immediately asked for <u>forgiveness</u> from Allah. Muslims believe that we are only responsible for our <u>own sins</u>.

2) The spirit <u>Iblis</u>, who was given the title <u>Shaytan</u> ('adversary' or 'enemy'), tempts humans from the right path. He was the one disobedient spirit who refused to <u>bow down</u> to the newly-created Adam. Iblis believed he was superior to man.

"[Allah] said, 'What prevented you from prostrating when I commanded you?' [Satan] said, 'I am better than him. You created me from fire and created him from clay.' [Allah] said, 'Descend from Paradise, for it is not for you to be arrogant therein. So get out; indeed, you are of the debased.' " Qur'an 7:12-13

3) Muslims believe that Iblis <u>whispers</u> lies into people's ears to try to get them away from following Islam. But by focusing on Allah's message in the Qur'an, Muslims can <u>protect</u> themselves from the schemes of Iblis.

Would you Adam and Eve it...

So, the big differences between the faiths are: Christians believe we're <u>born</u> with sin and only Jesus Christ can save us, Muslims believe Shaytan <u>leads</u> us into sin and Jews believe that any sins we commit are down to <u>us</u>.

The Problem of Evil

What believers mean by the 'problem' of evil is <u>why</u> there is evil in the world and how we should <u>respond</u> to it.

Evil can be either Human-Made or Natural

Evil and suffering can be divided into <u>two types</u>:

HUMAN-MADE (OR MORAL) EVIL

1) This is when suffering is brought about by the <u>cruel</u> actions of <u>people</u>.

2) This includes things like murder, war, rape and torture.

3) The person causing the evil is able to make a <u>choice</u> about what is morally <u>right or wrong</u>.

NATURAL EVIL

1) This kind of evil, and the suffering that comes with it, is <u>caused by the world</u> in which we live and is <u>no-one's 'fault'</u>.

2) This includes things like disease, floods, earthquakes and hurricanes.

3) However, many <u>recent natural disasters</u> may have been caused by <u>human interference</u> in the natural world, raising the question of whether that makes those events human-made.

Many people have tried to <u>define</u> evil and work out <u>what</u> it is or <u>where</u> it comes from. Some have argued that <u>human-made</u> evil is a <u>psychological phenomenon</u> that some people are <u>more prone to</u> than others.

Evil can Lead People to Question their Faith

1) <u>Evil</u> and <u>suffering</u> may lead some people to <u>question</u> their belief in God — or even to <u>reject</u> their faith.

2) This might be because they can't believe that a God who is <u>good</u> would <u>allow</u> such things to happen, or because they feel that their <u>prayers</u> are not being <u>answered</u> (i.e. they think God <u>could</u> help, but <u>doesn't</u>).

3) Other people might argue that God can't be very <u>powerful</u> if he is <u>unable</u> to prevent suffering (i.e. God <u>can't</u> help, even if he wanted to).

Christians Disagree about the Problem of Evil

1) Some Christians would argue that most evil comes about because of how we <u>humans</u> act. After the Fall (p.23) we have the <u>choice</u> to do evil — and it is our responsibility not to.

2) Some Christians think that evil is <u>necessary</u> for there to be free will — without the choice of doing wrong what freedom is there? They believe that there has to be evil in the world for it to be <u>possible</u> for us to <u>do good</u> — really doing good things requires that we could have acted differently. If we could only do good, how virtuous would we really be?

3) Many Christians believe that all the suffering in the world will in the end come to good — that God has a <u>plan</u> in which we must have <u>faith</u>.

I'm all part of the GRAND PLAN, darling.

Judaism says Suffering Requires a Human Response

1) The <u>Book of Job</u> in the <u>Hebrew Bible</u> contains a key Jewish idea on evil. Job endures <u>terrible suffering</u> of all kinds and he <u>questions</u> God. In the end Job comes to the conclusion that God is <u>all-powerful</u> and knows what he is doing — and that suffering must be <u>accepted</u> because we can't really <u>understand</u> the world or <u>God's plan</u>.

2) Judaism teaches that we have <u>free will</u> and are able to <u>choose</u> what we do (like Adam and Eve — see page 23). But we are prone to making <u>mistakes</u>.

3) Most Jewish thought doesn't seek to explain the presence of evil, or try to explain away the problem of evil. Many Jews believe that evil requires a <u>human response</u> rather than a philosophical explanation — i.e. being available to help people who are the victims.

It'll be a problem for you too if you don't learn it...

Bad things happen — it's a fact of life, I'm afraid. It's no wonder that this stuff is a problem for religious believers. But most faiths try to tackle evil constructively and to help the victims of natural and moral evil.

The Problem of Evil

The Holocaust — the Nazis' Extermination of Jews

1) Towards the end of the 18th century, Jews living in Europe began to face greater persecution than ever before from nationalists who thought that Jewish blood was watering down their own racial identity.

2) This hatred of Jews became known as anti-Semitism, and spread through many countries — especially France, Germany, Austria and Russia. The fact that many Jews regarded themselves as loyal citizens of these countries didn't stop this from happening.

3) Later, during the 1920s, Germany faced huge economic problems. The National Socialist (Nazi) Party seemed to offer solutions. It pinned the blame for the country's problems on 'non-Aryan' people (i.e. those who weren't considered 'pure Germans') living in Germany — especially the Jews.

4) In 1933 its leader Adolf Hitler became Chancellor of Germany, and laws began to be passed that gradually deprived the Jews of their citizenship rights.

5) Eventually Hitler introduced the Final Solution — the plan to wipe out the Jews completely. Throughout World War II (1939-1945) concentration camps and extermination camps were built in the countries under Nazi control. Huge numbers of Jews perished here in gas chambers.

The Holocaust Caused Jews to ask "Where was G-d?"

The Holocaust posed very serious spiritual problems for Jews — they had to find answers to questions like:

If G-d exists, and he is good, and all-powerful, how could he have allowed such terrible suffering?
If we are the 'chosen people', how could G-d have let six million of us be wiped out?

Jews have come up with many responses to this type of question:

1) Some Jews have concluded that there is no G-d.

2) Some have concluded that if G-d does exist, he either doesn't care, or is powerless to intervene.

3) Some Jews say that the Holocaust, and all suffering, is a test of faith — if good people always got the best things in life, everyone would be good for the wrong reasons.

4) Some Jews say that G-d could intervene to stamp out evil if he chose to. However, he gave all human beings free will and refuses to override this even when it is abused. Also, it would be impossible for G-d to 'destroy all evil people' because no-one is completely evil or completely good.

5) Some Jews regard all those who died in the Holocaust as martyrs for the faith, and see their martyrdom as 'sanctifying the name of G-d'.

6) Some say the most important thing is to keep practising Judaism, or else Hitler will have won.

Islam says we have the Choice...

1) Islam teaches that humankind was created with free will. Therefore, people can choose to follow Allah, or choose to do wrong. Without the possibility of choosing wrong there would be no free will.

2) Allah allows Shaytan (see p.23) to tempt humankind — we have free will so can choose whether to give in to temptation or not. It's a test of faith.

3) Islam teaches that if we choose to act against the will of Allah we will have to answer for that wrongdoing on the Day of Judgement.

4) Everything that happens is part of Allah's plan. Allah has good reasons for allowing evil, including natural evil, to occur — even if that isn't immediately apparent to us.

5) Evil also gives people the chance to do good. It's up to us to be good and help those in need. If we ourselves are afflicted by evil, Muslims believe we must meet it with patience and faith.

Not the cheeriest couple of pages in the book, for sure...

Yes, it'd be nice if RS was all fun and laughter, but unfortunately we have to deal with the bad stuff too. And not just any bad stuff, but some of the worst bad stuff there's ever been. This can be a real problem for a lot of religious people. Make sure you understand the key responses to evil for the religion(s) you're studying.

Christianity, Islam & Judaism

Coping With Suffering

Different people <u>cope</u> with suffering in different ways.

Many Christians Cope with Suffering through Prayer

1) <u>Praying</u> for and <u>helping</u> those who suffer is a key part of many <u>faiths</u>.

2) Roman Catholics and Orthodox Christians often pray for a <u>saint</u> to <u>intercede</u> with God on behalf of someone who's suffering. These are called '<u>intercessory prayers</u>'. In other Christian traditions, prayers of intercession for others are addressed <u>directly</u> to God.

3) Christians also pray for God's <u>help</u> in <u>accepting</u> suffering as part of his plan for the world — whether it's their <u>own</u> suffering or that of others.

4) Many Christians believe that it is when we <u>struggle</u> and <u>suffer</u> that we are <u>closest</u> to Jesus, who suffered and died for us.

5) One argument that Christians make for accepting suffering is that life — including all its pain — must be <u>worthwhile</u> if God, in the form of Jesus, chose to come down and <u>share it</u> with us.

6) Many Christian organisations, e.g. Christian Aid, work to alleviate suffering by offering <u>practical help</u>.

Jews Believe that Good can come out of Suffering

1) Like many Christians, Jews may also <u>respond</u> to suffering and evil through <u>prayer</u>.

2) The <u>Jewish</u> approach often stresses the idea that <u>good</u> can come out of terrible suffering. Suffering can bring people <u>closer</u> to <u>each other</u> and <u>closer to God</u>.

3) It also allows people to make <u>sacrifices</u> for other people and draw on their <u>inner strength</u>.

4) The following passage is taken from the <u>Midrash</u> (a collection of Rabbinical commentaries on the Tenakh or Jewish Bible):

   "*Not to have known suffering is not to be truly human.*"

   It suggests that suffering is simply a part of the <u>human experience</u> and, therefore, must be <u>accepted</u>.

Only Allah knows why he tests us in these ways.

The Qur'an says "We Will Surely Test You"

The following passage is taken from the Qur'an 2:155-156:

"*And We will surely test you with something of fear and hunger and a loss of wealth and lives and fruits, but give good tidings to the patient, who, when disaster strikes them, say, 'Indeed we belong to Allah, and indeed to Him we will return.'*"

This is remarkably similar to the moral of the Book of Job — (see page 24).

These are just some ways people cope with suffering. There are differences in belief and tradition <u>within</u> each religion.

1) The idea here is that <u>suffering should be accepted</u>. Muslims believe that, despite suffering in <u>this life</u>, there will be <u>joy in the next</u> as Allah is <u>compassionate</u>.

2) <u>Prayer</u> is one way of <u>coping</u> with evil and suffering. Prayers for Allah's help or forgiveness are called <u>du'a</u>. If people pray for <u>forgiveness</u> when they have <u>done wrong</u> they will be <u>forgiven</u>. One of the ninety-nine names of Allah is <u>Al-Ghaffar</u> — <u>The Forgiver</u> (see page 3).

3) Muslims believe that those who are <u>suffering</u> should be <u>treated compassionately</u> by others. Many <u>Muslims work to help</u> those who are suffering.

"Will I be forgiven?" — "Best ask the Ghaffar"...

Christianity, Judaism and Islam all have similar ideas about this stuff: 1) Suffering is part of God's plan, so it should be accepted. 2) You should always try to help others who are suffering, through actions and prayer. 3) If you pray for forgiveness after doing something wrong, God/Allah will be merciful and will forgive you.

Sources of Moral Guidance

General & Christianity

A moral code is a list of what someone believes to be right and wrong. Different people use different sources of moral guidance. For most religious people, the first place to start is sacred texts.

People Look for Moral Guidance in Different Places

Religious people look in various places to find the 'truth' about what's right, and what God wants.

SACRED TEXTS Believers most commonly look to sacred texts (e.g. the Bible, the Qur'an or the Torah and Talmud) for moral guidance. Some people claim that the religious texts were written for a society with different values, and should be interpreted to suit the times. Others argue that they're the Word of God and so must be obeyed to the letter. (There's loads more about sacred texts on pages 32-34.)

THE EXAMPLE OF TEACHERS/PROPHETS Religious people may also look at the lives and actions of teachers like Jesus and Muhammad to guide them along the right path (more about that later).

CONSCIENCE Your conscience is that little voice in your head telling you what's right or wrong. Some believers argue that this is the voice of God, so we should listen to it very carefully and always trust what it's telling us. Others say that it's just the result of your upbringing — e.g. your parents' opinions, things you've read or heard, religious teachings... If this is true, then your conscience is only as trustworthy as the things it's based on. Some people believe that your conscience has to be schooled in the teachings of your faith, or it might lead you astray.

A little voice told Kevin it was wrong...

"My conscience is clear, but that does not make me innocent. It is the Lord who judges me." 1 Corinthians 4:4

Jesus Set an Example for Christians Today

Jesus Challenged Laws and Traditions in the Name of Love

1) Jesus's Jewish opponents often accused him of breaking religious laws — for example, he healed people on the Sabbath when Jews were not supposed to do any work.

2) Jesus thought the Jewish authorities had missed the point of God's law, and that the 'spirit' of the law was more important than the 'letter'. He also criticised the Pharisees for allowing ritual and tradition to become too important, e.g. in Mark 7:1-22 he challenges 'ritual washing' and 'unclean' things.

3) In fact, he taught that your motivation was even more important than your actions — being angry with someone could be as bad as killing them (Matthew 5:21-22).

4) Above all else, Jesus wanted his followers to love. When asked which was the most important commandment, he gave a pretty neat answer that summed up his beliefs...

"Love the Lord your God with all your heart and with all your soul and with all your mind and with all your strength... love your neighbour as yourself." — Mark 12:30-31

Jesus Set an Example of Self-Sacrifice

1) Christians believe that in his willingness to suffer and die on their behalf, Jesus set an example which they themselves should be prepared to follow. In Mark 8:34 Jesus says, *"If anyone would come after me, he must deny himself and take up his cross and follow me."*

2) In dying on the cross, Christians believe Jesus paid for all the sin of mankind. The Bible teaches that God is merciful, but he is also just, so our sins have to be paid for.

3) Christians believe that everyone who has died will be judged. Most Christians believe that only those that have followed Jesus's teachings, and have behaved morally (or have repented and sought forgiveness for any immorality) will enter Heaven as a result of his sacrifice.

And the moral of the story is — erm... revise... yep, that's it...

In practice, most Christians base their moral decisions on lots of different sources. But respect and love are the basic principles of Christianity, and they're a good place to start when you're looking for answers.

Judaism & Islam

Sources of Moral Guidance

Observant Jews believe they should live in a way that's pleasing to G-d — this means obeying the 613 mitzvot.

Morality Matters in Judaism

The most famous mitzvot (commandments) are the Ten Commandments (see Exodus 20) — but they're not the only ones. There are 613 mitzvot in total, which can be divided up in different ways...

> 248 of the mitzvot are positive, telling Jews what they should do.
>
> 365 are negative, telling them what they shouldn't be doing.

> Ritual mitzvot are about Jews' relationship with G-d.
>
> Moral (ethical) mitzvot are about Jews' dealings with other people.

> The first four of the Ten Commandments are ritual mitzvot, and the last six are moral mitzvot.

> The singular of mitzvot is mitzvah.

1) Observant Jews think it's vital to live by a moral code, and will generally regard a moral individual as someone who combines religious observance with concern for other people.

2) In deciding how to behave, Jews look first to the Torah, then to the Talmud (there's more about these on p.33), then to the wider body of traditional Jewish teaching. But an individual Jew can always ask someone who knows more about these things than they do.

> The word 'mitzvah' is sometimes translated as a 'good deed'.

3) Jews realise that no one can live by all 613 mitzvot all of the time. But they believe that G-d is merciful and will always forgive someone who is truly sorry for his sins. Yom Kippur (see page 15) reminds Jews of this every year.

4) For Reform Jews the buck stops with the individual conscience. They're expected to use all the traditional sources of authority on moral behaviour, but in the end they must decide for themselves what's right.

5) Orthodox Jews tend to believe that the correct moral judgements are to be found by sticking as close as possible to traditional Jewish teaching — from the Torah, the Talmud or from other respected sources.

Muslims Follow the Qur'an and Muhammad's Example

1) According to the Qur'an, the prophets bring Allah's message so that people know how to behave.

2) Allah's mercy and compassion mean he can't just leave us to mess up our lives. So Allah gives messages to angels, who then pass on his words to prophets (or rasuls).

3) Allah sent many prophets as messengers, maybe because we seem to forget the plot quite quickly. But Muhammad was the last prophet (the 'seal of the prophets'), and Allah revealed the Qur'an to him.

4) As Allah's last prophet, Muslims regard Muhammad as a very moral, trustworthy man, that they should try to be like. Collections of his sayings (Hadiths) are a source of moral and spiritual guidance for many Muslims — particularly Sunni Muslims.

5) The Sunnah is a record of Muhammad's life and actions. It's seen as the model for a correct Muslim life.

Khalifah — Taking Responsibility in Allah's Name

1) Muslims believe that they have a duty to obey Allah.

2) Allah has laid down rules for living a moral life in the Qur'an (e.g. rules on dress, money and food), so any Muslim who doesn't obey those rules is disobeying Allah.

3) Muslims believe that they will pay for any disobedience on Judgement Day, when Allah will judge us on the basis of our actions.

4) Muslims also believe they they have been appointed khalifah (vice-regents or trustees) of the Earth. This is the idea that while we're on Earth we should take responsibility for the world in Allah's name, and make it the sort of place he wants it to be. This sometimes means applying the teachings of the Qur'an to new situations, and relying on our conscience to tell us what's right and wrong.

613 — that's an awful lot of rules...

So sacred texts will tell you generally how you ought to behave, but you need to use your conscience too.

Practice Questions

Hmmm... evil and suffering — there's a nice cheery topic to start a new unit on. But many religious believers think suffering is just part of the human experience — and it's how we respond to that suffering that shows what kind of person we are. It would be easy to be a good person if the world was perfect.

In a perfect world, there probably wouldn't be any exams either. Ah, well — life's tough sometimes. Have a go at all these questions. Make sure you can do them all. If there are any you get stuck on, have a look back through the section and then try again. If you can't do these, you really are going to suffer come exam time.

1) What is:
   a) evil?
   b) the Fall? *(Christianity)*
   c) sin?
   d) Shaytan? *(Islam)*
   e) conscience?

   These are worth just 1 mark each, so keep your answers short and sweet.

2) a) What is meant by 'original sin'? *(Christianity)*
   b) State two things that Christians/Jews/Muslims believe about the nature of evil.
   c) Give two examples of suffering in the world.
   d) What is meant by a 'moral code'?
   e) Give two sources of moral guidance for a Christian/Jew/Muslim.

   2 marks — 2 points. It's easy to get carried away with some of these questions, but you haven't got time to write an essay in the exam.

3) a) Describe the nature of Satan/Iblis according to Christians/Jews/Muslims.
   b) Describe the difference between natural and moral evil.
   c) How might acceptance help people cope with suffering?
   d) Describe the role of conscience in making moral decisions.

   These questions are worth up to 3 marks, so you'll need to go into a bit more depth.

4) a) Explain how some Christians/Jews/Muslims respond to the problem of evil in the world.
   b) Explain how different Jews respond to the Holocaust. *(Judaism)*
   c) Explain what Christians/Jews/Muslims might do to help them cope with suffering.
   d) Explain why Christians/Muslims try to follow the example of Jesus/Muhammad. *(Christianity) (Islam)*
   e) Explain why most Christians/Jews/Muslims try to lead a moral life.

   For these questions, you're marked on the quality of your writing, as well as what you know. They're worth 6 marks each, so you need to spend a bit of time on them.

5) Read the following statements:
   a) "We are only answerable for our own sins."
   b) "God/G-d/Allah cannot prevent suffering."
   c) "Suffering should be accepted as the will of God/G-d/Allah."
   d) "Moral judgements should be based only on sacred texts."

   Discuss each statement. You should include different, supported points of view and a personal viewpoint. You must refer to a religion in your answer.

   These questions are worth 12 marks each. So take your time, structure your answer carefully, and give as many different sides of the argument as you can.

The Form and Nature of Revelation

There are <u>loads of ways</u> people claim to <u>experience God</u>. These religious experiences allow people to 'know' God as he reveals himself to them.

Revelation — *God Reveals His Presence*

God can <u>reveal</u> his presence in <u>different ways</u>...

Revelation of *Sacred Texts*

Christians, Muslims and Jews believe that the <u>truth</u> about the world, and their <u>rules</u> for good behaviour were <u>revealed</u> to them by God. These revelations were written down in the <u>scriptures</u> — the <u>Bible</u> (p.32), the <u>Torah</u> (p.33) and the <u>Qur'an</u> (p.34).

The Qur'an is believed to be the <u>direct word of Allah</u>, revealed to Muhammad by the angel Jibril (Gabriel) and written down <u>word for word</u> by scribes (there's more about that on the next page). So the Qur'an is seen as a <u>direct revelation</u>.

Most Christians and Jews believe their scriptures were <u>divinely inspired</u>. That is, that God revealed himself to the <u>prophets</u> and <u>apostles</u>, who then wrote the sacred texts based on those experiences. So most people view the Bible and the Torah as <u>indirect revelation</u>.

Revelation through *Mystical and Religious Experiences*

The revelation of the scriptures was something that happened a long time ago, but religious people believe that God still reveals himself today, through <u>religious experiences</u>.

1) <u>PRAYER</u>
Prayer is an attempt to <u>contact God</u> directly. It usually involves <u>words</u> and can be thought of as a <u>conversation</u> with God. A person might feel the presence of God in an <u>answered prayer</u>, e.g. if an ill person they pray for is cured, or if they are filled with a sense of <u>inner peace</u> or <u>wonder</u>.

2) <u>MEDITATION</u>
In meditation, a believer <u>clears</u> his or her mind of distractions and <u>focuses on God</u>. This could involve repetitive <u>prayer</u>, <u>reading scripture</u> or <u>fasting</u>. It doesn't need to be in a place of worship — you can <u>meditate anywhere</u>. Meditation can result in <u>visions</u> or <u>voices</u> as the believer draws closer to God.

3) <u>MIRACLES</u>
Some people believe miracles occur today (e.g. healing at Lourdes, statues of the Virgin Mary crying blood), and that these miracles show God's <u>power</u> and <u>presence</u> (see page 5).

4) <u>RELIGIOUS ECSTASY</u>
These experiences range from <u>singing</u>, <u>dancing</u>, <u>shaking</u> or <u>crying</u> during worship to '<u>speaking in tongues</u>' (unknown languages), having <u>visions</u> or <u>prophesying</u> (speaking a message from God).

5) <u>SACRAMENTAL RITUALS</u>
These are the rituals in which <u>Christians</u> believe God makes his presence felt <u>directly</u>. According to Roman Catholics, there are seven sacraments — baptism, confirmation, reconciliation, Eucharist (Holy Communion), ordination, marriage and anointing the sick. For example, <u>in Holy Communion</u>, Catholics believe that the <u>bread and wine</u> actually <u>become</u> Christ's body and blood (called <u>transubstantiation</u>) and this reveals the presence of God.

Revelation through the World

Many believers feel that God reveals himself constantly in the world through <u>numinous experiences</u>.

This describes an experience that inspires <u>awe</u> and <u>wonder</u>, where someone can <u>feel God's presence</u>, e.g. a <u>beautiful sunset</u>, a <u>wild sea</u> or a <u>butterfly's wing</u> might convince you there must be a creator.

"I've got a revelation here for a Mr Smith..."
Revelations, eh... Wow. I mean, just imagine. It's just <u>mind-blowing</u>...

The Form and Nature of Revelation

Jesus Doesn't just Reveal God — He is God

1) Most Christians believe that the Jewish prophets spoke for God (see below), but they believe that God revealed himself fully in the person of Jesus. Christians believe he was both fully God and fully human.

2) Jesus's teachings were written down during his life and passed on in the Gospels. They include the Sermon on the Mount (Matthew 5-7) which many believe is Christ's most important revelation.

3) In his death and resurrection, Christians believe Jesus showed his divine nature to man.

Jews Believe G-d Spoke to them through the Prophets

In Judaism, prophets are believed to speak for G-d among the people. A whole section of the Tenakh (p.33), called Nevi'im, is made up of the words of prophets such as Isaiah, Jeremiah and Ezekiel. According to Jewish traditions there have been many thousands of prophets, although not all have been remembered. Here are two of the most important:

Abraham (between 2000 and 1800 BCE)

1) Jews call him Avraham Avinu ('our father Abraham'). He was the first of the patriarchs — the founders of Judaism.

2) Unlike his neighbours in Ur, he believed in one god. G-d told him to leave Ur and go to Canaan, also known as The Promised Land, The Holy Land, and later Israel. G-d promised this land to his descendants.

3) G-d made a covenant with Abraham which forms the basis of Jewish beliefs. G-d promised Abraham many descendants that G-d would never abandon. In return they had to be circumcised. The covenant was renewed at Mount Sinai with the giving of the Torah. Jews regard their history as the story of the covenant.

Moses (around 1300 BCE)

1) Abraham's descendants had to leave Canaan and escape to Egypt because of a famine. In Egypt they multiplied and the Egyptians made them slaves for 400 years.

2) With the help of G-d's direct intervention (sending the Ten Plagues on the Egyptians) Moses then led the Jews to freedom — an event called the Exodus. Their journey back to Canaan took 40 years.

3) On the way back, G-d revealed the Ten Commandments (Exodus 20) to Moses. Moses is regarded as the greatest of the prophets, and is traditionally believed to have been the divinely inspired author of the Torah (see p.33)

Muslims Believe there were Many Prophets

Muslims believe that there have been many thousands of prophets in history, across all nations, revealing the nature of Allah and calling people to him. They believe that Muhammad was the final and greatest of these prophets. Muslims have special reverence for Ibrahim (Abraham), Musa (Moses) and Isa (Jesus) who are seen as delivering special messages from Allah to their people, but whose messages later got added to and distorted.

Muhammad was the Final Prophet

Muhammad was around 40 years old when he was called to receive Allah's final revelation.

1) While he was meditating in a cave on Mount Nur, Allah sent the angel Jibril (Gabriel) to him.

2) Although Muhammad was initially frightened, his wife Khadijah helped him realise that Allah was calling him to be a prophet.

3) Muhammad received many revelations from Allah, over 20 years. The Qur'an (p.34) records the exact wording of these revelations.

This was the message that the Prophet Muhammad had to take to the people of Makkah:

i) People were to worship one God, Allah — not many gods.
ii) People were to listen to him, because he was Allah's Prophet.
iii) People were to conduct their business honestly, and to look after the poor.
iv) If they did not do all this, they would be sent to Hell.

Christianity

Sacred Texts — The Bible

The <u>Bible</u> is a <u>collection</u> of books in different styles and languages written over a period of at least 1000 years. It's also the Christian <u>Scripture</u> — meaning that for Christians, it's <u>sacred</u>.

The Bible — the Old and New Testaments

The Bible's divided into two main parts — the <u>Old</u> and <u>New Testaments</u>:

THE OLD TESTAMENT

The Old Testament is the <u>Jewish Scriptures</u> (i.e. it's considered sacred by Jews). Written in Hebrew and Aramaic, its 39 books include the <u>Creation</u> story, the books of the Law (<u>Torah</u>), the <u>10 Commandments</u>, various <u>histories</u> of Ancient Israel, <u>prophecy</u>, <u>poetry</u> and <u>psalms</u>.

THE NEW TESTAMENT

The New Testament is the specifically <u>Christian</u> part of the Bible. Written in Greek in the 1st Century CE, its 27 books include the <u>4 Gospels</u>, the <u>Acts</u> of the Apostles (describing the early years of Christianity), 13 <u>letters</u> by St Paul (giving advice about the Christian life), 8 letters by other early Christian leaders, and the <u>Revelation of St John</u> — an apocalyptic vision.

The 4 Gospels are Matthew, Mark, Luke (called the <u>Synoptic Gospels</u>, as they are all very similar stories of Jesus), and John (which portrays Jesus in a very different way). The word 'Gospel' means 'good news', and the Gospels tell the good news about Jesus Christ.

The Bible is used as a Christian Faith Guidebook

Christians accept the Bible as <u>authoritative</u> in forming their beliefs and guiding their actions.

1) Christians believe the Bible offers directions for living a <u>moral</u> life. It presents Jesus Christ as our example for <u>godly</u> living, and teaches that we best love <u>God</u> by showing love to <u>others</u>.

2) Both the Old and New Testaments (but especially the New) include <u>rituals</u> for <u>worship</u>, large parts of which are still included in <u>modern</u> worship services (e.g. <u>Holy Communion</u> and <u>baptism</u>).

3) The faith of the Roman Catholic Church is based largely on the <u>Scriptures</u>, but Catholic <u>tradition</u> and the <u>Magisterium</u> (i.e. the teaching of the Pope, his cardinals and bishops) are also very important. The Protestant Churches claim their authority mainly from the Scriptures.

4) Different groups of Christians <u>interpret</u> the Bible in different ways:

1️⃣ **Literalism** Many Christians believe that pretty well everything in the Bible is <u>literally</u> true, e.g. Jesus really did 'walk on water'.

◀ *Some people argue that there are <u>contradictions</u> in the Bible, and so it's impossible for everything in it to be <u>literally</u> true.*

2️⃣ **Fundamentalism** This is a form of literalism. Fundamentalists believe that it's wrong to <u>question</u> anything in the Bible, since it was <u>dictated</u> by God.

3️⃣ **Conservative View** This view is probably the most common among Christians. They believe that the Bible was <u>inspired</u> by God but not dictated — the writers' own interests also come through. Readers must use their intelligence and the guidance of the Holy Spirit in order to understand the writers' intentions.

4️⃣ **Liberal View** Liberals believe that pretty well everything in the Bible can be interpreted '<u>symbolically</u>', e.g. Jesus didn't really 'walk on water' — the story has some other 'spiritual' meaning.

The Bible has been Influential for Centuries

1) There are many different <u>versions</u> of the Bible in use today, and loads of <u>translations</u> into other languages.

2) The <u>Gospels</u> (which contain the teachings of Jesus) are <u>central</u> to Christian faith.

3) Christians often meet to <u>study</u> the Bible and to <u>pray</u>, and it's also read for <u>guidance</u>, or as an act of <u>devotion</u> towards God.

The Bible — sells more than any revision guide...

The Bible has profoundly affected <u>countless</u> lives (e.g. the saints, missionaries, campaigners for social change), and arguments over its interpretation continue to be a <u>legal</u> matter in some countries — e.g. courts in the USA have had to legislate recently on whether schools should teach the Bible's Creation story as <u>fact</u> or <u>fable</u>.

Sacred Texts — The Torah & Talmud

Judaism

The 'Jewish Bible' is the <u>Tenakh</u> (often just called the <u>Torah</u>). This is basically the same as the Christian <u>Old Testament</u>, except that it's in a different order. The word 'TeNaKh' even helps you remember what's in it.

The Tenakh — its Letters tell you its Contents

T = Torah (Instructions / Law / Teachings)

The <u>Torah</u> is the first <u>five</u> books of the Bible (<u>Genesis</u> to <u>Deuteronomy</u>). It contains 613 commandments (<u>mitzvot</u>) which Jews are supposed to live by. Jews regard the Torah as the holiest part of the Tenakh, as it was given to Moses directly by G-d.

But many people use the word 'Torah' to refer to the <u>whole</u> Tenakh.

N = Nevi'im (Prophets)

This collection of books is divided into two. The <u>Former Prophets</u> trace the history of the <u>Israelites</u> after the death of Moses. The <u>Latter Prophets</u> contain the words of <u>Isaiah</u>, <u>Jeremiah</u>, <u>Ezekiel</u> and <u>12 Minor Prophets</u>. All these men encouraged the Jews to keep their part of the <u>covenant</u>, and their words are believed to have been <u>inspired by G-d</u>. However, the books in the Nevi'im do not have as high a status as the Torah.

K = Ketuvim (Writings)

This is a hotch-potch of other stuff, chiefly the three 'P's: <u>Psalms</u> (hymns), <u>Proverbs</u> (wise and witty sayings), and <u>Philosophy</u>. This part of the Tenakh is less authoritative than the others.

Torah means Different Things to Different People

Some Jews use the word 'Torah' to refer to the whole <u>Tenakh</u>. Others use it to mean the enormous body of <u>teachings</u> which grew up over the centuries to explain how the Torah should be applied in a <u>changing world</u>. Although some of these teachings were originally passed on by word of mouth (and were known as the <u>Oral Torah</u>), they eventually they got written down in a number of <u>collections</u>:

① The Mishnah ('Learning' or 'Repetition')
This was a collection of <u>Oral Torah</u> written down by Rabbi Judah the Prince (roughly 200 CE). It ran to 63 volumes.

② The Gemara ('Completion')
This is an <u>extended commentary</u> on the Mishnah.

③ The Talmud (the Mishnah and Gemara combined)
Some Jews think that God gave the entire contents of the <u>Talmud</u> to <u>Moses</u>, so it has a very high status and authority.

④ The Codes
The Talmud was so huge that summaries had to be made. An important example is the <u>Mishneh Torah</u> written by <u>Maimonides</u> in 1167. Another is the <u>Shulchan Aruch</u> from the 16th century.

⑤ The Responsa
New questions arise as technology develops, so panels of rabbis meet to give '<u>responses</u>' to tricky questions, e.g. whether people should drive on the Sabbath.

Orthodox Jews Live Strictly by the Torah

1) <u>Orthodox</u> means 'right belief'. Orthodox Jews think that traditional Jewish beliefs and practices are still important <u>today</u>. Roughly 80% of <u>British</u> Jews belong to Orthodox synagogues, though not all are equally <u>observant</u>.
2) Orthodox Jews believe that the Tenakh and Talmud are of <u>divine origin</u>, and are to be followed to the letter.

Progressive Jews Interpret the Torah Less Rigidly

1) <u>Progressive Jews</u> apply the Torah to <u>modern life</u> in a very different way. They believe that it's merely people's <u>interpretation</u> of the word of G-d.
2) They consider the <u>moral</u> commandments <u>binding</u> (although open to <u>interpretation</u>), but the <u>ritual laws</u> can be <u>adapted</u> or <u>abandoned</u> in response to changes in society. In <u>Britain</u>, there are two Progressive movements: <u>Reform</u> and <u>Liberal Judaism</u>.

Islam

Sacred Texts — The Qur'an

Muslims believe the Qur'an is the most important book in the world, as it records the exact words of Allah. They call these words revelations, because they were revealed by Allah to the Prophet Muhammad.

The Qur'an is Treated with Respect

For Muslims, the Qur'an is...

1 A COMPLETE RECORD OF ALLAH'S WORDS: The Prophet never forgot any revelations, and his followers recorded them at once, and learned them by heart.

2 A TOTALLY ACCURATE AND UNCHANGED RECORD The early Caliph (Muslim ruler) Uthman made sure there was only one version and that it was completely correct.

3 A COMPLETE GUIDE TO ISLAMIC LIFE The Qur'an says what Muslims must believe, and how they must live, in order to get to Paradise. In the Qur'an, Allah tells Muslims what they need to know, so that they can please him. Since Muslims believe the Qur'an came direct from Allah, they trust it completely. Basically, if the Qur'an says 'Do this,' then a Muslim must do it.

4 ALWAYS IN ARABIC Allah gave the Qur'an to the Prophet Muhammad in Arabic. If you read it in another language, you might not get the proper meaning. So all Muslims must learn Arabic to be sure they are reading the real Qur'an.

Because the Qur'an is so important, Muslims treat it with great respect. Many Muslims will:

1) keep their Qur'an wrapped up to keep it clean,
2) wash their hands before touching it,
3) keep it on a higher shelf than all other books,
4) place it on a special stand when they read it.

The Qur'an is also read during private and public prayers, so Muslims get to know it really well. In the month of Ramadan, it's read from beginning to end during worship at the mosque.

The Qur'an is Divided into 114 Surahs

1) The Qur'an is organised into 114 Surahs (chapters).
2) The Surahs are arranged in order of length — longest first, shortest last (apart from Surah 1, the Fatihah, which is a short and punchy statement of central beliefs).
3) Each Surah is made up of Ayat (verses).
4) Most Surahs begin with the Bismillah — an Arabic phrase meaning 'In the name of Allah, the Entirely Merciful, the Especially Merciful'. This means that when Muslims start to read any Surah, they are reminded of the mercy and kindness of Allah.

The Hadith and the Sunnah are also Important Texts

Muslims also pay a lot of attention to the guidance and example they get from the following:

1 THE HADITH — the sayings of the Prophet Muhammad that were not part of the Qur'an. These were Muhammad's words, not Allah's.

2 THE SUNNAH — the actions and way of life of Muhammad.

Because Muhammad was chosen by Allah to be his last Prophet, they regard him as a very remarkable man, and pay special attention to his words and actions.

Are you surah you've learnt all of this...

When Muslims read the Qur'an, they're learning about what Allah's like, how he relates to humans, and how to live the way Allah wants so they can get to Paradise and thus avoid the 'unpleasantness' of Hell. Basically, if it's in the Qur'an, it's important. And if it's important in Islam, it may well be in the Qur'an.

Practice Questions

That section was little short of revelatory (boom, boom). Ah, the old ones are the best, but it's worth remembering that some sort of experience of God/G-d/Allah is at the heart of all three religions. Whether it's the direct revelation that the founders of the faiths experienced, or in quiet moments of private prayer, it really is the source of all the other stuff in the book.

And this is where we reveal how much you've remembered and understood. Go through the questions (for those religions you're covering) and try to answer them all. If you can't answer any go back through the section to find the answer. Keep repeating this little ritual till you can answer all the questions without checking back.

1) What is:
   a) revelation?
   b) meditation?
   c) literalism? *(Christianity)*
   d) the Hadith? *(Islam)*
   e) the Oral Torah? *(Judaism)*

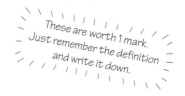
These are worth 1 mark. Just remember the definition and write it down.

2) a) What is meant by a religious experience?
   b) State two important religious texts for Jews/Muslims. *(Judaism) (Islam)*
   c) State how two different groups of Christians/Jews interpret scripture. *(Christianity) (Judaism)*

Get a couple of facts down in short order and move on. Don't get bogged down with 'em — they're only worth 2 marks.

3) a) Describe the role of Jesus in the revelation of God to the Christians. *(Christianity)*
   b) Describe the role of Muhammad in the revelation of Allah to the Muslims. *(Islam)*
   c) Describe the role of Abraham in the revelation of G-d to the Jews. *(Judaism)*

3 marks for these questions. Make sure you cover the key details without going into essay mode.

4) a) Explain how it is that many Christians/Jews/Muslims feel God/G-d/Allah reveals himself to believers today.
   b) Explain how some Christians/Jews/Muslims regard their scriptures.
   c) Explain why some Christians/Jews don't believe that everything that is written in their scriptures is literally true. *(Christianity) (Judaism)*
   d) Explain why Muslims believe that everything in the Qur'an is literally true. *(Islam)*
   e) Explain why Christians believe that Jesus was more than a prophet. *(Christianity)*

You can start to stretch your legs with these ones — they're worth a whole 6 marks. You'll be judged on how good your writing is for these questions, too.

5) Read the following statements:
   a) "We don't need any new revelations."
   b) "God/G-d/Allah can be found outside scripture."
   c) "Scripture is the literal word of God/G-d/Allah."
   d) "Sacred texts can't help to solve today's problems."

   Discuss each statement. You should include different, supported points of view and a personal viewpoint. You must refer to a religion in your answer.

These are worth 12 marks each — that's the same amount as the rest of the questions combined. Aim to give a structured essay-style answer that covers both sides of the argument.

Christianity, Judaism, Islam & General

Origins of the World and Life

No one saw exactly how the Earth came to be like it is... but science and religion both have their theories.

Scientific Arguments — There are Two Main Types

COSMOLOGICAL THEORIES — How the Universe came into being

Chief amongst these is the Big Bang theory. It says that the Universe began in an explosion of matter and energy. Matter from this explosion eventually formed stars, planets and everything else. The Universe still seems to be expanding today — important evidence for this theory.

EVOLUTIONARY THEORIES — How living things came to be like they are today

In 1859, Charles Darwin published 'On the Origin of the Species'. In this book he argued that all life on the planet originated from simple cells. Life evolved (gradually changed) over millions of years into a huge variety of forms. According to this theory, we evolved from apes — not from Adam and Eve.

These theories are at odds with many religious arguments. However, if you don't take everything in the Bible or Torah literally, scientific and religious ideas can exist in harmony. Science tells us how, religion tells us why.

Religions have their Own Ideas about all this...

Christian Ideas

1) Christian and Jewish ideas about Creation come from the same scriptures, and so are quite similar.

2) Christian thinking is based on the idea that God created everything. If the Bible is taken literally, the process took six days, and humankind didn't evolve from apes, but is descended from Adam and Eve.

3) However, it can also be viewed as a parable, or as a symbolic description of a more gradual evolution. This means it's possible to believe in the Bible and science.

For example, the Bible says things were created in the following order — the heavens (i.e. space) and Earth, the atmosphere, land and sea, and then plants, animals and people. This is pretty much the same order as scientists believe things appeared. So the timescale is different (millions of years rather than six days), but the general idea is the same.

4) In 1996 the Roman Catholic Church accepted the Big Bang theory — definitely a significant acceptance of science.

"In the beginning God created the heavens and the earth." Genesis 1:1

Yeah, not bad. I reckon I deserve a day off.

Jewish Ideas

1) Orthodox Jews, who see the Torah as the word of God and so literally true, would find it difficult to accept scientific arguments about creation. God is believed to have created the world in six days. And humanity is believed to have started with Adam and Eve.

2) Reform Jews might argue that Creation as described in the Torah is more a way for us to understand, not an explanation of, how it happened.

Islamic Ideas

1) Muslims believe that Allah created the world and everything in it.

2) However, unlike Christianity and Judaism, descriptions of creation in the Qur'an are not entirely at odds with science. Islam does not really compete with the Big Bang theory or Darwinism. In fact, scientific theories are supported by passages such as this.

"Have those who disbelieved not considered that the heavens and the earth were a joined entity, and We separated them and made from water every living thing? Then will they not believe?" Qur'an 21:30

In the beginning, God created exams...

Albert Einstein once said that if you see something beautiful or amazing, you are seeing the work of God. Yeah, well... what did thicky Einstein know... But whether the Universe came to be this way through chance or design is a key question in the science versus religion debate. (More about that on page 4.)

People and Animals

Religions usually say be nice to other people. But what about squirrels...

Christianity says Animals come Below People

According to the Bible, God created the world, mankind was created to populate it, and animals were created for the use of mankind. But animal rights issues are still of interest to many Christians. For example...

i)	Animal experimentation (e.g. vivisection),	iv)	Hunting,
ii)	Factory farming,	v)	Genetic modification and cloning,
iii)	Destruction of natural habitats (e.g. deforestation), leading to extinction,	vi)	Zoos and circuses,
		vii)	Vegetarianism.

1) One of the major issues for Christians is whether animals have souls or not. If they don't, then some people will argue that God created us as superior to them, and that animals are here for our use.

"...Rule over the fish of the sea and the birds of the air and over every living creature that moves on the ground." Genesis 1:28

2) Christianity teaches that we should treat animals with kindness, but that they can be used to benefit mankind (as long as their suffering is considered). It's also thought that excessive money should not be 'wasted' on animals when human beings are suffering. So humans are very definitely 'on top', with animals below.

3) But some Christians point out that as everything is interdependent, our treatment of animals reflects on us. Indeed, the Church of England teaches that the medical and technological use of animals should be monitored 'in the light of ethical principles'.

4) The Roman Catholic Church is more likely to tolerate things like animal experimentation, but only if they bring benefit to mankind (e.g. if the experiments lead to the development of life-saving medicines).

5) Certain denominations are generally opposed to any ill-treatment of animals — especially for our pleasure. For example, the Society of Friends (Quakers) are particularly likely to frown upon zoos, animal circuses, hunting and the wearing of fur.

6) Unlike some other religions, there are no specific food laws to be followed in Christianity. So vegetarianism (not eating meat) and veganism (not eating or using any animal products) are a matter for individual Christians to decide about.

The Bible tells us that Jesus ate fish, and as a Jew he would have eaten meat at certain festivals.

Judaism and Islam have Similar Views

JUDAISM

1) The Noachide Laws (laws given to Noah after the Flood) clearly forbid cruelty to animals. Animals are here to help us, and not to be abused. There are many stories in the Torah that demonstrate care for animals.

2) In Judaism, if meat is to be eaten, the animal must be slaughtered in a 'humane' fashion. This involves cutting the throat of the animal with a very sharp blade to bring about a quick death.

Deuteronomy 5:14 says that animals deserve a day off on the Sabbath, just like people.

"...you shall not do any work, neither you... nor your ox, your donkey or any of your animals..." Deuteronomy 5:14

3) Experiments on animals may be tolerated if they result in a benefit for mankind, but only as a last resort. Cruel sports (e.g. bull fighting) are seen as an abuse of God's creatures.

"...when you slaughter, slaughter in a good way. So every one of you should sharpen his knife, and let the slaughtered animal die comfortably." Prophet Muhammad (Sahih Muslim)

ISLAM

1) Khalifah is the idea that we're responsible for the Earth — khalifah means vice-regent, or trustee (see p.28).

2) Cruelty to animals is forbidden, as is their use simply for our pleasure.

3) Muslims believe in demonstrating mercy and compassion for all living creatures, and animals used for meat must be slaughtered humanely.

So it's OK to kill them as long as you eat them afterwards...

I bet you thought it would all be simple. You thought I was just going to say something like, 'all religions say be nice to furry things'. Well, they do — to an extent. But this is the page where animal experimentation and stuff comes in, which means benefits for people at the expense of animals. Which complicates things.

Environmental Issues

Environmental problems today mean the Earth is suffering. Sadly, many of these problems are man-made...

Our Small Planet has some Big Problems

The environmental problems facing the world include...

i) Global warming (and the Greenhouse Effect),
ii) Deforestation,
iii) Extinction of animal and plant species,
iv) Pollution (leading to problems like acid rain),
v) Scarcity of natural resources.

1) Developed countries are the worst (but not the only) polluters. Competition means that businesses often feel forced to put profit before the welfare of the planet — if they don't, they may not survive.

2) Some governments look more to short-term benefits than long-term care for the planet.
They may say they're trying to do the best for their people, and that people should be our first priority.

3) Governments in developing nations often claim that they're only doing now what richer countries did in the past, and that it's hypocritical for richer countries to tell them what they should be doing.

4) There are things we can do, as individuals, to help minimise our impact on the environment.
For example, recycling helps conserve natural resources, and walking more, using public transport or using alternative energy resources (e.g. solar power) could reduce greenhouse gas emissions from fossil fuels.

Religious Ideas about the Environment — 'Stewardship'

Christianity, Islam and Judaism have pretty similar ideas when it comes to looking after the Earth. All three religions teach that God has put us in charge of the Earth, but that we must do our duty responsibly.

CHRISTIANITY

1) Christians of all denominations believe that God gave us the Earth, but expects us to care for it — this idea is called 'stewardship'. We have no right to abuse God's creation — we must act responsibly.

2) There's pressure on governments and companies to sell goods and services, even at the expense of the environment. Although it can be difficult to balance taking care of the Earth with providing for humankind, this is what Christians believe we must try to do.

"We have a responsibility to create a balanced policy between consumption and conservation." Pope John Paul II, 1988

3) Christianity teaches that everything is interdependent (i.e. everything depends on everything else), so driving species of animal or plant to extinction, or harming the planet, eventually ends up harming us.

4) Christian organisations such as CAFOD, Christian Aid and Tearfund are concerned with putting this responsibility into practice. They put pressure on governments and industry to think more about how we are abusing the planet.

"You made him [humankind] a little lower than the heavenly beings and crowned him with glory and honour. You made him ruler over the works of your hands; you put everything under his feet" Psalm 8:5-6

"The earth is the Lord's, and everything in it, the world, and all who live in it; for he founded it upon the seas and established it upon the waters." Psalm 24:1-2

JUDAISM

1) Jews also believe in the concept of stewardship. Concern for the natural world is often seen as being at the heart of Jewish teaching.

2) God's creations should remain as he intended, and we have no right to abuse them. Everything is interdependent, with trees being seen as particularly important.

3) Jews also believe that as custodians, they're responsible for making the world better — this is called Tikkun Olam ('perfecting the world'). Tikkun Olam isn't just about the environment — it's a general ideal that includes helping the poor, and behaving morally.

"The Lord God took the man and put him in the Garden of Eden to work it and take care of it." Genesis 2:15

ISLAM

1) Muslim teaching on environmental issues is very similar to that of Judaism — we are seen as trustees (khalifah).

2) At the Day of Judgement we'll have to answer for any ill-treatment of the planet and its resources.

3) The Earth is seen as being a product of the love of Allah, so we should treat it with love.

Dr Abdullah Omar Nasseef stated at the 1996 World Wide Fund for Nature conference that, "His [Allah's] trustees are responsible for maintaining the unity of his creation, the integrity of the Earth, its flora and fauna, its wildlife and natural environment."

Look after the planet — or it's eternal damnation for you, my friend...

Again, the ideas of all three of these religions are very similar — we're looking after the place for the 'big man'.

Practice Questions

And now.... the end is near... it's time to face... the final questions...

You know the drill by now. Try all the questions — for any you can't do, look back through the section to find the answer and then have another go. Keep trying until you can do them all.

1) What is:
   a) evolution?
   b) Creation?
   c) vegetarianism?
   d) khalifah? *(Islam)*
   e) stewardship?

Have a look in the glossary at the back of the book if you're struggling with these 1-mark definitions.

2) a) State two ways in which animals are used by humans.
   b) State two environmental problems faced by the world.
   c) What is meant by 'Tikkun Olam'? *(Judaism)*

These 2-mark questions just check that you know the basic facts about the religions you're studying.

3) a) Briefly describe the Big Bang theory of the origin of the universe.
   b) Briefly describe Christian/Muslim/Jewish teachings about the origins of the world.
   c) How does Darwin's theory of evolution explain the existence of humanity on the Earth?
   d) Briefly describe Christian/Muslim/Jewish teachings about the origins of humanity.
   e) How could you reduce your impact on the environment?

Don't get carried away with these questions. They're only worth 3 marks each, so you don't have to write an essay. Just get the facts down.

4) a) Explain why some Christians/Muslims/Jews do not accept scientific explanations about the origin of the world and humanity.
   b) Explain Christian/Muslim/Jewish teachings about the importance of animals in relation to humans.
   c) Explain Christian/Muslim/Jewish attitudes towards the proper treatment of animals.
   d) Explain why most Christians/Muslims/Jews believe they should take care of the planet.

You get more marks for these if you structure your answer clearly, and get your spelling, grammar and punctuation spot on. They're worth 6 marks in the exam.

5) Read the following statements:
   a) "God/G-d/Allah created the universe and everything in it."
   b) "It doesn't matter how we treat animals."
   c) "The world is not ours to destroy."
   Discuss each statement. You should include different, supported points of view and a personal viewpoint. You must refer to a religion in your answer.

For these big 12-mark questions, you have to give a balanced argument, with good reasons to back up all your points. But don't forget to put your <u>own opinion</u> in somewhere.

Do Well in Your Exam

General

You've learnt all the <u>facts</u> — now it's time to get those <u>grades</u>.

You'll have a <u>1-Hour Exam</u> on Each Unit

1) For the <u>Philosophy 1</u> exam you'll have a choice of questions covering <u>Belief about Deity</u>, <u>Religious and Spiritual Experience</u>, and <u>End of Life</u>.

2) For the <u>Philosophy 2</u> exam you'll have a choice of questions on <u>Good and Evil</u>, <u>Revelation</u> and <u>Science</u>.

3) For each exam you have to answer <u>two questions</u> — you'll also have the choice of which <u>religion</u> to focus on for each question. You have to pick your questions from <u>different topics</u> — you can't just answer the same questions for different religions.

4) Each question is split up into <u>five parts</u>. You have to answer <u>all</u> the parts of the questions you pick.

You get Marks for <u>What you Know and How you Express it</u>

In GCSE Religious Studies there are two <u>Assessment Objectives</u> — these are the skills you'll need to show to get marks in the exams. You get <u>half</u> your marks for each.

> 1) The first gives you marks for <u>describing</u> and <u>explaining</u> what you <u>know</u>.
> 2) The second gives you marks for using <u>arguments</u> and <u>evidence</u> to <u>explain</u> and <u>evaluate</u> what you and others think.

Jock was unable to express his detailed knowledge of the world's major religious traditions — he couldn't get a grip on a pen with his flippers.

There's an <u>Easy Mark</u> for <u>Knowing What Things Mean</u>

Question (<u>a</u>) is worth 1 mark, which you'll get for defining what an <u>important term means</u>. These questions only carry 1 mark so keep your answer <u>short</u> and <u>to the point</u> — but make sure you define the term <u>properly</u>. Learn the terms that relate to each unit from the glossary.

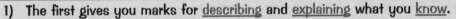

a)   What is fasting?   (1 mark) | Going without food and/or drink for a set time.

> Try to answer this kind of question in one sentence.

You need to <u>Know the Basics</u>

Question (<u>b</u>) is worth <u>2 marks</u>, which you'll get for making a couple of short points.

b)   Give two elements of a Muslim funeral rite.   (2 marks)

After the person has died, the body is washed and wrapped in a clean white shroud. The body is buried facing Makkah.

> You don't need to go into depth for these questions — just a couple of details.

> The question may not ask specifically for two points, but as there are two marks try to get two facts down.

It's not all <u>Religion</u>

The exam can have questions on <u>anything</u> covered in the course. That includes the bits that <u>don't directly relate</u> to religion.

c)   What can people do to reduce the damage they do to the environment?   (3 marks)

> For parts (a), (b) and (c) you don't need to worry about connecting your points together.

People can recycle paper and glass, which reduces the amount of natural resources they consume. Using public transport instead of the car reduces the amount of greenhouse gases put into the atmosphere. Installing a solar panel means that people can reduce their reliance on electricity produced using fossil fuels.

> Make sure you've got examples for all the things you've covered.

Do Well in Your Exam

General

For questions (d) and (e) you're still marked first and foremost on your <u>understanding</u>, and the <u>facts</u> you remember about the religion in question. However, you can get a <u>better mark</u> if you use <u>better English</u> — so write your answers in <u>proper sentences</u> and <u>paragraphs</u>.

You'll have to Explain...

d) Explain Jewish beliefs about suffering.   (6 marks)

> In Judaism suffering is seen as an integral part of life. It says in the Midrash that "Not to have known suffering is not to be truly human."
> Jewish people believe that although there is terrible suffering in the world, it will come to some good as part of G-d's plan. We cannot know what our suffering is for, we can only have faith that G-d has a reason for it.
> Jewish people believe that G-d gave people free will. This means that much suffering is not caused directly by G-d, but is the fault of people making bad choices and doing bad things.

Don't forget to explain and develop your points.

It doesn't hurt if you can remember a good quote.

...and you'll have to Discuss...

Half the marks for each question will come from part (e). This is where you'll be given a <u>statement</u> that you'll have to <u>discuss</u>. To get all the marks you have to <u>refer</u> to the <u>specified religion</u> as well as including your <u>own opinion</u>.

e) "Scientific discoveries make the existence of God less likely."
   Discuss this statement. You should include different, supported points of view and a personal viewpoint. You must refer to Christianity in your answer.   (12 marks)

> I do not believe that scientific discoveries prove that there is no God. I would argue that the scriptures, which scientific discoveries have made difficult to believe in literally, should be interpreted symbolically.
> Many Christians do not find the scientific explanation of creation a problem. They would argue that although the universe was not created exactly as described in the Bible, it does not mean that God was not involved. They believe that we should look for the spiritual lessons of the creation story, rather than treating it as if it were a scientific theory about the universe.
> Some Christians, known as creationists, reject scientific theories about evolution and geology, which go against the literal meaning of scripture. For them, no scientific discovery can make God's existence less likely, as any discovery that threatened to do so would be rejected.
> People who believe that science has made the existence of God less likely, would argue that one of the most important proofs of God has been disproved. The argument from design — that the world is so complex it had to have a designer — could be said to have been disproved by the theory of evolution which shows how complexity could have arisen without being externally guided.
> Some people would argue that the Big Bang theory proves that God did not create the world, and that questions about what was before the universe do not even make sense. They would argue that this removes the need to believe in God as a 'first cause'.
> I would argue that believing in God makes more sense when based on religious experiences, such as a feeling of the numinous in prayer, than on the foundation of a literal understanding of scripture.

Make a totally clear reference to the religion you're discussing.

Discuss different perspectives.

Try to look at both sides of the argument.

To get the best marks you must include your own personal response.

Thou shalt write clearly...

As much as you may know every little fact that pops up in this book, a large chunk of how well you do in exams will come down to, well..., how good you are at exams. Make sure you spend enough time reading through these pages, and enough time practising doing exam-style questions under timed conditions. It'll all pay off in the end.

Philosophy 1 Glossary

The purple definitions are only for those studying Christianity. The blue ones are for Judaism only. The green ones are for Islam only. The rest are for everyone.

agnosticism	A belief that it's impossible to know whether or not there's a god. Not knowing if God exists.
atheism	A complete denial of the existence of a god.
bereavement	The loss of someone close to you through their death.
Church	The community of all Christians — also often used to refer to a particular community, e.g. the Roman Catholic Church. A place of worship is a church with a lower case 'c'.
cremation	The burning of dead bodies.
death	The point at which the body stops functioning. When life finishes.
fasting	Not eating and/or drinking for a set time. Used in religion for atonement or to focus the mind on spiritual matters.
funeral	The rites associated with disposing of the dead, usually through burial or cremation.
a god	A divine being. The subject of reverence or worship for a religion.
halal	Allowed according to Muslim food laws. Forbidden things are haram.
Holy Spirit	The third person of God in the Christian Trinity. Believed by some to be the force of God acting in the world.
icon	Paintings of saints and other religious figures, used in the Orthodox Christian tradition to help believers pray.
kosher	Allowed according to Jewish food laws. Forbidden things are terefah (torn).
Lent	The period spent remembering Christ's 40 days of fasting in the desert. Some Christians go without luxuries during Lent. It ends with Easter Sunday.
life after death	The religious belief that after death some sort of life continues, and the form that life takes.
menorah	A seven-branched candlestick used for Hannukah — a symbol of Judaism.
miracle	An event believed to be the work of God, that can't be explained by the laws of science.
monotheism	The belief that there is only one god. Christianity, Judaism and Islam are all monotheistic.
mosque	A Muslim religious building or house of prayer.
Nicene Creed	The Christian statement of belief in the Trinity.
ninety-nine names	The list of names Muslims believe are the best for describing Allah — as revealed in the Qur'an.
omnipotent	Having unlimited powers — all things are possible.
prayer	An attempt to contact God directly, often in the form of a conversation.
religious symbol	Religious symbols are objects which represent aspects of religious belief.
resurrection	Being brought back to life after death. This could be the resurrection of the body or the soul.
Rosary	A string of beads used by Catholics, and the set of prayers that goes with them.
Sawm	The Muslim obligation to fast during daylight hours through the month of Ramadan.
Siddur	The Jewish prayer book, which gives details of set prayers for specific times.
soul	The non-physical part of a person. The part of us that some people believe continues to live after our physical death.
Synagogue	The main Jewish religious building.
Tawhid	Belief in the oneness and incomparability of Allah. The opposite of this is Shirk.
the Trinity	The Christian belief that God exists in three persons — Father, Son and Holy Spirit.
wudu	The ritual washing of exposed parts of the body three times before prayer in Islam.

Philosophy 2 Glossary

The purple definitions are only for those studying Christianity. The blue ones are for Judaism only.
The green ones are for Islam only. The rest are for everyone.

the Bible	The Book of Holy Scripture for Christians. Contains the Old Testament (the Hebrew Bible) and the New Testament.
conscience	An inner feeling of what's right and what's wrong. Some believers think that your conscience is the 'voice of God'.
creation	The act of making something, or the thing that has been made. In Religious Studies, this usually refers to the creation of the Universe by God/G-d/Allah.
evil	The bad things that happen in the world and the suffering they cause, or the force that makes bad things happen.
evolution	The process by which life changes form over millions of years to adapt to its environment.
the Fall	Adam and Eve's breaking of God's commandments, and expulsion from the Garden of Eden.
the Hadith	Islamic scripture containing a collection of things the Prophet Muhammad said.
khalifah	The idea that we are responsible for the Earth. It literally means 'trustee' or 'vice-regent'.
literalism	The belief that everything in religious scripture is literally true.
meditation	A form of religious discipline that involves clearing the mind of distractions — often by focusing on a prayer.
moral evil	Suffering caused by human beings, e.g. war, murder, rape, torture.
natural evil	Suffering caused by the world we live in, e.g. disease, floods, earthquakes, hurricanes.
Oral Torah	Jewish teachings passed down orally and not included in the Tenakh. These oral traditions were recorded in the Talmud.
original sin	The idea that, after the Fall, all humans are born in a state of sinfulness, which we require God's help to overcome.
the Qur'an	The main scripture of Islam. Believed to be the direct word of Allah, as given to Muhammad, as the final and perfect revelation.
revelation	An experience that reveals a god's presence to a believer.
Satan	In Christianity, the force for evil, seen as a figure tempting people to do wrong. Appears in Jewish scripture but is not a part of modern Jewish thought. Also known as the Devil.
scripture	The texts associated with a particular religion, i.e. the Bible, the Torah and Talmud, the Qur'an and Hadith. Often considered to be sacred or divinely inspired.
Shaytan	The title given to Iblis, the rebellious spirit in Islam who is allowed by Allah to tempt people away from Islam by whispering lies in their ears.
sin	An act that breaks a religious law, i.e. when God's teaching is disobeyed.
stewardship	Taking care of the Earth as custodians of creation, so that it can be passed on to the next generation.
the Talmud	The collection of Jewish scriptures made up of the Mishnah and the Gemara, which explains the Jewish teachings in the Torah. Some believe it was given to Moses by G-d.
the Tenakh	Jewish scriptures made up of the Torah, the Nevi'im and the Ketuvim
Tikkun olam	The belief that Jews are responsible for 'perfecting the world'. This includes looking after the environment, taking care of the poor, and behaving well.
the Torah	The first five books of the Tenakh, the most important collection of Jewish scripture, believed to have been given by G-d to Moses. Can also be used to mean the entire Tenakh or the entire body of Jewish traditional teachings which developed over the centuries.

Index